What Others Are S₂

"My husband and I just attended your (apraxia) workshop in Victoria. **Wow**!"

— Helena, mom, British Columbia

"I just wanted to thank you for writing such amazing books. . . . I never have found any R method to be as helpful. **Your books have improved and enhanced my therapy** more than any continuing education course that I've taken since I graduated 11 years a go! I will highly recommend your books!"

— Kimberly, SLP, Washington

"Your work has helped support mine and the families with children with AOS tremendously. **I've incorporated much of what you teach with success**."

— Monique, SLP, web comment

"**My staff and I love your stuff**—very practical. . . . Keep it coming."

— Nancy, SLP, New Jersey

"I just received your *Becoming Verbal with Childhood Apraxia* book a couple of weeks ago and am **singing your praises to everyone!**

— Karen, mom, Missouri

"**I really admire your work**. . . . Your R ideas have helped immensely this year with my clients! . . ."

— JoAnne, SLP, Wisconsin

Apraxia
Uncovered
Seven Stages of Phoneme Development

PAM MARSHALLA

MSL
Marshalla Speech and Language

© 2005 by Pamela Marshalla. All rights reserved
Printed in United States

Marshalla Speech and Language
11417 - 124th Avenue Northeast
Kirkland, WA 98033
www.pammarshalla.com

ISBN 0-9707060-9-X

To …

Drs. David Kimbrough Oller and Marsha Zlatin Lauffer, who taught me to think about the way infants vocalize.

Special thanks to the hundreds of speech and language pathologists who provided the speech samples presented throughout this text.

Contents

Seven Stages of Phoneme Development

Children with severe expressive speech disorders have one great universal need: They must learn to speak intelligibly with correct consonants and vowels. *Apraxia Uncovered* teaches just that. The seven stages concept has evolved through thirty years of speech and language therapy with countless hundreds of children who display a wide variety of severe expressive speech disorders. The stages represent an integration of research on infant vocal development with standard practices in articulation, phonological and oral-motor therapy into a program designed to stimulate phoneme development in children with severe expressive speech delay or disorder.

Children with apraxia and dysarthria do not respond well to traditional speech therapy methods and procedures. These children seem unable to figure out how to produce specific phonemes, and the sounds they do produce emerge slowly, even painstakingly.

Children with apraxia or dysarthria need a different approach to acquire speech. They need a therapy that actually teaches them how to make their speech mechanism function correctly. If they can figure out how to work their speech mechanism, they can use that skill to produce more phonemes and intelligible speech.

A child spends his first few years of life discovering how his body works. He figures out how to sit, stand, grasp, release, hit, kick, poke his fingers into holes, turn knobs, pull off and on his clothing, eat, drink, climb, slide, swing, and countless other actions. One of these other actions is speech, the coordinated activity of respiration, phonation, resonation, and oral-motor action. While he is discovering how his body works, a child also is discovering every action necessary to make speech sounds. By the time he has reached three years of age, the average child has learned how to coordinate his body in every possible way in order to produce all the consonants and vowels of his native language. He can put these sounds together to form words and he can put words together to construct phrases and sentences.

Speech is a movement that, like all movements, is learned over time. Most children learn speech movements naturally as they grow and develop. But some children need specific training to help them learn these movements. *Apraxia Uncovered* provides such training for children with apraxia or dysarthria. Through this program, children learn specific respiration, phonation, resonation, and articulation movements—speech actions—necessary to produce all the consonants and vowels of English. This program also guides children in the application of these phonemes to intelligible words and phrases.

This material has been written for speech and language pathologists and others interested in the development of speech in children with apraxia and dysarthria. Sound and word examples in this book are presented in phonetic transcription. However, the examples given in the audio material makes these samples comprehensible by parents, teachers, and other professionals.

This material assumes basic knowledge about apraxia and dysarthria. However, simple definitions are offered here for clarity.

Apraxia can be defined as a nonlinguistic sensorimotor disorder of articulation characterized by difficulty in planning movements for speech. In other words, the child with apraxia knows what he wants to say but cannot figure out how to make his speech system function in ways that would result in specific sounds or sound sequences. The result is the very slow onset of speech and very slow acquisition of new speech sounds.

Dysarthria can be defined as a speech production problem that is the direct result of central or peripheral nervous system disorder. Children with dysarthria know what they want to say and they go ahead and say it. But the sounds and words they make are distorted, twisted, or bent. Dysarthria in the early stages can seem like apraxia because of a severe lack of phoneme development. Children can be both apraxic and dysarthric.

Children with apraxia or dysarthria are slow to acquire speech and difficult to understand. Still they want to communicate. Sometimes an augmentative form of communication is chosen to facilitate functional communication. The seven stages program does not disavow the advantages that augmentative communication systems bring to these children. Children who are nonverbal or minimally verbal can benefit greatly from the use of pictorial, orthographic, handsign, gestural, and technological communication systems. Augmentative communication systems such as these should be taught at the same time that the seven stages program is being used to stimulate phoneme development. The seven stages program also is beneficial for children who need no such augmentative communication services.

There are many approaches to the development of expressive speech. Traditional articulation therapy, phonological therapy, oral-motor therapy, and manual cueing systems all are useful in facilitating expressive speech and specific phonemes. The seven stages approach does not negate the value of these methods. The seven stages provide a framework in which these other tried-and-true methods can be placed. Simply put, the seven stages pull all these procedures together into a comprehensive developmental framework, providing a clear path of phoneme development. It teaches us how to organize our articulation, phonological, and oral-motor therapy for children with severe expressive speech disorder.

The Seven Stages
The seven stages of our program are *preparing, speechifying, honing, sequencing, solidifying, advancing,* and *finish-*

ing. These seven stages unfold from beginning to end throughout the course of time. Each stage represents one developmental platform of expressive speech acquisition. See table 1.

TABLE 1. THE SEVEN STAGES OF PHONEME DEVELOPMENT

1. PREPARING: Getting the voice ready for speech
2. SPEECHIFYING: Making utterances sound speech-like
3. HONING: Zeroing in on non-vocalic consonants differentiated by place
4. OSCILLATING: Creating primitive sequences with reciprocating oral movements
5. SOLIDIFYING: Establishing basic syllable constructions
6. ADVANCING: Leaping beyond simple syllable constructions
7. FINISHING: Incorporating the most difficult articulation skills

Advancement through the seven stages is marked by periods of fast and slow skill acquisition. Fast progress is made as children leap forward into their next developmental stages. Slow progress is made as children spend time learning all the skills required within their new stage. The slow periods of advancement can seem like stagnation or even failure. But therapists, parents, and teachers alike should be assured that their child is still making progress. The child is shoring up and broadening his current level of skills. He is stalling for a purpose. Stalling in a stage is a way to ensure that all the skills within that stage are mastered. This effort assures that the child actually can and will make the necessary leap to the next subsequent stage. A slow period gives a child the experience and confidence he needs to leap forward into the next developmental stage. It ensures that he will succeed at every level of the program.

The seven stages represent major milestones learned on the path of phoneme acquisition. These stages should be regarded with flexibility because, as is true of all developmental explanations of growth, there is overlap of one stage and another. Further, clients with expressive speech disorder do not always follow an expected plan of maturation. They follow their own path of development, often learning difficult skills before easier ones. The seven stages help us understand how to push skills further along on the developmental path, and at the same time identify gaps in the learning process that, when filled, can allow a fully intelligible speech production system to emerge.

The Action Skills of Each Stage

Each of the seven stages of phoneme development consists of unique skills called *action skills*. Action skills are respiratory, phonatory, resonatory and articulatory movements that alter vocal production. Action skills are the foundational units that actually allow children to discover how their speech mechanisms work. Children acquire new action skills during each stage, and each stage is complete when the action skills of that stage have been gained and mastered. The action skills are listed by stage on table 2. Each will be described in the text and in the lecture material.

TABLE 2: ACTION SKILLS BY STAGE

Stage	*Action Skills*
1. Preparing	A. Voicing
	B. Prolonging
	C. Differentiating
	D. Posturing
2. Speechifying	A. Projecting
	B. Pitching
	C. Intoning
	D. Pulsing
	E. Laughing
3. Honing	A. Vibrating
	B. Occluding
	C. Releasing
	D. Popping
	E. Fricating
	F. Vowelizing
4. Oscillating	A. Jaw Babbling
	B. Silent Sequencing
	C. Lip Babbling
	D. Tongue Babbling
	E. Classic Babbling
	F. Advanced Babbling
5. Solidifying	A. Embedding
	B. Closing
	C. Duplicating
	D. Diminutizing
	E. Diphthongizing
	F. Shortening
6. Advancing	A. Jargoning
	B. Word Jargoning
	C. Whispering
	D. Tripling
	E. Enclosing

7. Finishing
A. /w/-Clustering
B. Syllabifying
C. Glide Clustering
D. Postvocalic /s/-Clustering
E. Prevocalic /s/-Clustering
F. Stridency Overgeneralizing
G. 3-Consonant Clustering
H. Advanced Clustering

Specific Vocalizations

Acquisition of each action skill results in the emergence of *specific vocalizations*. A specific vocalization is a unique prespeech or speech sound. For example, one of the action skills a child gains in the honing stage is to release occluded voiced raspberries. As a result of gaining this action skill, the child learns to say /b/, /d/, and /g/. Phonemes /b/, /d/, and /g/ are the specific vocalizations that emerge during the honing stage.

Each action skill contains a number of specific vocalizations that are acquired in their respective stages. These details will emerge and become clear throughout the written and lecture material. Readers are strongly urged to practice each specific vocalization as the program unfolds. Adults who produce these sounds purposefully will understand this material far better than those who don't, because their learning will be multisensory. The unfolding process of vocal development will become clear in the process. The audio material provides ample opportunity for listeners to imitate, hear, and feel these vocalizations.

Facilitation Techniques

The description of each action skill is followed by suggestions for facilitating the skill. It is assumed that readers possess basic knowledge about articulation, phonological, oral-motor, and feeding therapy, so explanations of specific methods are not given. For example, the general suggestion to "incorporate techniques to increase lip strength" is given, but the specific methods to do so are not. Readers are referred to the resources listed in the back for further reading on these topics.

Phonemes

Children should be able to produce all the phonemes—vowels, diphthongs, and consonants—of standard North American English by the end of this program. These phonemes are summarized in tables 3, 4, and 5.

TABLE 3. THE VOWELS OF ENGLISH

Category	Vowel	Sample Word*
Front	/i/	beet
	/ɪ/	bit
	/e/	bait
	/ɛ/	bet
	/æ/	bat
Back	/u/	boot
	/ʊ/	book
	/o/	boat
	/ɔ/	bought
	/ɑ/	box
Central	/ʌ/	but
	/ɚ/	bird

TABLE 4. THE DIPHTHONGS OF ENGLISH

Diphthong	Sample Word*
/ɑi/	bite
/ɑu/	bout
/ɔi/	boy
/iu/	beauty

TABLE 5. THE CONSONANTS OF ENGLISH

Category	Consonant	Sample Words*
Stops	/p/	pie, upper, cap
	/b/	boy, rubber, cab
	/t/	toy, utter, hat
	/d/	dog, udder, mad
	/k/	car, baker, back
	/g/	go, beggar, dog
Nasals	/m/	mad, hammer, thumb
	/n/	know, inner, man
	/ŋ/	Ngu, song, singer
Glides	/w/	watch, power, cow**
	/l/	lady, caller, till
	/y/	yam, player, hay**
	/r/	run, errand, car†
Hissing§	/f/	phone, offer, laugh
	/v/	vase, oven, glove
	/θ/	thumb, cathedral, math
	/ð/	that, other, bathe
	/s/	scene, kisser, bus
	/z/	zoo, buzzer, was
	/ʃ/	shoe, usher, bush
	/ʒ/	television, beige
	/tʃ/	chew, butcher, march
	/dʒ/	jump, badger, forge
	/h/	hat, behind

Writing an IEP

Apraxia Uncovered can be used to construct a child's individual educational program (IEP). Goals and objectives can be written that represent stages, action skills, or specific vocalizations.

Samples in the Text

All the word and phrase pronunciation samples chosen for the text come from the author's direct clinical experiences and from examples provided to the author by other professional speech and language pathologists across the United States and Canada. Samples were collected from 1975 through 2004. They have been acquired from children six months through twelve years of age who represent the full spectrum of intelligence and neuromuscular abilities.

Endnotes for Tables

* There are a number of spellings for most phonemes. For example, the sound of /f/ is represented by *f, ff, ph,* and *gh* as in *fun, offer, telephone,* and *enough.* Since our concern in this text is for pronunciation and not spelling, the words selected for tables 3, 4, and 5 illustrate many but not all of these spelling variations. Readers should refer to an introductory phonetics text (see References) or to a dictionary for complete spelling variations of each phoneme. Dictionaries usually present this information in the pronunciation tables.

** Considered a vowel in the final position.

† Considered a vocalic /r/ in the final position.

§ The term *hissing* has been chosen to represent all fricative and affricate sounds whether designated as a sibilant, a strident, or neither. This simple designation allows us to lump together /f/, /v/, /θ/, /ð/, /s/, /z/, /ʃ/, /ʒ/, /tʃ/, /dʒ/, and /h/ into one category. This single designation helps us in two ways. It makes for ease in discussion and it better represents the way children actually learn to produce these sounds.

Stage 1
Preparing

Getting the Voice Ready for Speech

BY THE END OF THE FIRST STAGE, a child will be able to make sound, prolong it, and direct it through the mouth and nose. He also will be able to shape the mouth in basic postures. Through this process the child will learn seven specific vocalizations: /ŋ/, /m/, /n/, /ɑ/, /i/, /u/, and /o/.

ACTION SKILLS
- voicing
- prolonging
- differentiating
- posturing

ACTION SKILL 1A

Voicing

The most fundamental skill necessary for the production of speech is voice. Voice for speech is
made by setting the vocal folds into vibration during
exhalation. The first speech-like vocalization is called
the *quasi-resonant nuclei* (QRN). The QRN is a high,
mid, unrounded, nasalized vowel of short duration.
This is the sound made when the speech mechanism
does nothing but produce voice. Let's examine this
definition.

QUASI-RESONANT NUCLEI
- *High*: This is a reference to the jaw. The jaw
  is immobile. At rest, the jaw is relatively high.
  Therefore, in producing the QRN the jaw is
  characterized as high.
- *Mid*: This is a reference to the tongue. The
  tongue is immobile during production of the
  QRN. Since the QRN was first defined in ref-

erence to neonatal vocalizations, the tongue was described relative to the oral cavity as large. Thus, the tongue is bulbous and the middle sits high in the mouth.

- *Unrounded*: This term refers to the lips. The lips are unmoving—neither rounded nor retracted.
- *Nasalized*: This is a reference to the velopharyngeal mechanism. This mechanism is inactive during production of the QRN. Therefore, the sound is produced with a nasal quality.
- *Vowel*: The QRN essentially is a vowel. It is more vocalic than consonantal.
- *Short Duration*: The QRN is produced as a short pulse of sound. It is not prolonged.

Encouraging Voice

The first step in the facilitation of expressive speech is to find some way that encourages a child to produce his own voice. The second step is to find a way that directs a child's attention to his voice in such a way that he is motivated to produce more of it. We are not concerned with the specific sounds the child is producing at this stage. The treatment methods of this first action skill are applied to this skill and to most subsequent action skills. As such, they are described in detail here and are referenced regularly throughout the first part of the program. Modifications to these basic procedures are explained in each subsequent stage.

1. SPEECH ACTIVATION TOYS: Some toys dance and move about in response to the voice. There are several of these toys, including a butterfly who flaps its wings, a dinosaur band who rocks and rolls in response to sound, a parrot who repeats back a child's utterances, and others. These toys are fun for most children. A toy's antics encourage a child to make more voice in order to get the fun to continue. Many of these toys require a certain level of loudness before they will activate and some of our clients cannot produce that much voice. Therefore, devise some way to direct the child's voice directly to the toy and to make it louder. For example, have the child produce his voice into a tube that has one end placed at his mouth and the other at the toy, near the receiver.

2. KAZOOS: The kazoo is a great tool for stimulating vocal production because the kazoo only will sound when voice is directed through it.

3. FLEXIBLE TUBES: Flexible tubes help amplify a child's voice and direct it straight to his ear. Place one end at the mouth and the other at the ear. A child's voice will be carried directly to his own ear. It will be amplified and the airflow will tickle the child's ear. Amplification grabs the child's auditory attention, and the tickling sensation encourages him to make more sound. The child also may want to place one end at your ear to stimulate you in these ways.

4. FUNNELS: Funnels amplify voice like a megaphone. In fact, use a megaphone if you can find one. Pretend these funnels or megaphones are instruments. March around the room and make music with the voice through these tools.

5. SMALL ECHO CHAMBERS: Encourage the child to produce voice into large bowls, pots or boxes. These act as natural sound amplifiers. Also use a plastic Echo Mic.

6. LARGE ECHO CHAMBERS: Make voice in acoustically reverberating bathrooms, hallways, stairwells, and closets. Also make voice in large refrigerator or stove boxes. Make voice in other hiding spaces—kid's "forts," under blanketed tables, inside crawling tubes, etc. All these spaces and places amplify the voice and make listening to voice fun.

7. SYNCHRONOUS VOCALIZATIONS: Help a child recognize and pay attention to his own voice by making his sounds at the same time he does. Imitate whatever sound he is making and do so simultaneously, as if you were cooing or singing together.

8. MUTUAL IMITATION: Reflect a child's voice back to him by imitating his sounds immediately after he does. Wait for him to produce another sound, and then imitate it. Continue this back-and-forth process to create a dialogue of vocalizations.

9. SINGING: A child at this level is not ready for singing, *per se*, but pretending to sing is a great

way to facilitate active production of voice.
Allow the child to make any sound he wants
during the song. Use children's songs, songs on
the radio, and make up silly songs throughout
the day.

10. ROUGH HOUSE AND GROSS MOTOR PLAY: Some
children are very quiet unless engaged in
rough house or gross motor play. We can use
these to stimulate and encourage early vocalizations. Combine them with the synchronous voice and mutual imitation procedures
described above.

11. HORNS, WHISTLES, AND SIRENS: Horns, whistles
and sirens do not require the production of
voice to be sounded. Therefore, they are not
used to stimulate the voice required for this
action skill. However, the movement of air
into and out of the lungs is the basis of all
vocal production. Therefore, horns, whistles
and sirens are included here. Such blow toys
are used to help a child become aware of the
movement of air into and out of his lungs.
Once aware, blow toys are used to increase
volume of inhalation and prolongation of
exhalation. Some toys encourage only inhalation, some only exhalation, and others
both. Each blow toy should be analyzed for
the inspiration and expiration qualities it
encourages. Horns, whistles and sirens come
in a wide variety of shapes and sizes, and
each style requires a different amount of airflow and a different mouth shape to make it
sound. Some are easy to blow and others are

hard. Begin with the easy ones and progress to the hard ones. An inspiration and expiration spirometer is another excellent tool that can be used like a blow toy.

12. SENSITIVITY: Some children respond negatively to horns, whistles and sirens because of oral-tactile hypersensitivity. In this case, introduce these items at a pace the child can tolerate. Apply other methods to normalize sensitivity in the meantime.

13. ORAL STRENGTH: Some children cannot work a horn, whistle or siren because they haven't got enough lip movement or strength to wrap their lips around the mouthpiece. Employ other oral-motor and feeding techniques to increase these skills.

14. DIALOGUE: Engage in dialogue in such a way that the child is encouraged to use his spontaneous vocalizations in dialogue with you.

ACTION SKILL 1B

Prolonging

Once a child can make voice, his first development comes in the form of prolonging that sound. A child learns to prolong his QRN by inhaling more deeply and exhaling longer. Longer productions of the QRN catch his attention and motivate him to make more sound. Children typically enjoy the sensation of making voice because it stimulates the chest, throat, pharynx, mouth, and nose. This pleasure encourages them to make sound often, and they do so as a form of self-entertainment and calming.

Facilitating Prolongation

The key to prolonged vocal production is the ability to inhale more deeply, to exhale longer, and to sustain voice throughout the prolonged exhalation.

1. CONTINUE: Continue all voice and airflow stimulation activities as described in action

skill 1a. Encourage deeper inhalation and longer exhalation or voice production with each item.

2. PROLONGATION WHISTLES: Some whistles specifically encourage prolonged exhalation. The toy market carries an assortment of these ever-changing products.

   A. *Slide whistles* encourage a child to blow longer while he slides a moving piece back and forth to alter pitch. Encourage the child to make different sounds.

   B. *Rainbow blowers* require prolonged exhalation to keep their rainbow-colored string moving through the pipe. Encourage the child to keep the string going.

   C. *Frog blowers* encourage prolongation of exhalation in order to keep the frog's ball-shaped eyes afloat above its head. Encourage the child to keep the eyes up.

ACTION SKILL 1c

Differentiating

Once a child is able to prolong voice, he can begin to experiment with channeling the sound stream differentially through his mouth or nose. The velopharyngeal mechanism, located at the back of the mouth, controls the channel of oral and nasal airflow in the speech production system. Children seem to discover the velum by activating it antagonistically with the back of the tongue.

1. ORAL SOUND: Oral sound results when the velum and the back of the tongue move away from one another. The velum elevates upward to close off the nasal cavity, and the tongue-back lowers to allow sound to travel into and through the mouth.

2. NASAL SOUND: Nasal sound results when the velum and tongue move toward one other and when they articulate. The velum relaxes

toward the back of the tongue, and the tongue-back stretches up toward the velum. The nasal sound that results is /ŋ/. As such, /ŋ/ can be classified as the child's first consonant. Babies produce this sound naturally and easily because the size of a baby's tongue is large relative to the size of his oral cavity. Also, a baby at this stage will have poor head control and will spend most of his day supine or prone. In supine, the tongue naturally falls back toward the velum.

Facilitating Differentiated Oral and Nasal Sound

Experimentation with velar control is the key to differentiating oral and nasal sound.

1. CONTINUE: Continue all voice and airflow stimulation activities as described above.
2. MODIFICATIONS TO FLEXIBLE TUBES: Use the flexible tubes to accentuate the oral and nasal channels of airflow. Place one end of a tube at the child's nose. Place the other end at the child's ear. Have him listen to his nasal sound. Then switch the one end from the child's nose to his mouth so he can listen to his oral airflow. Alternate back and forth between nose and mouth to compare and contrast.
3. TERMINOLOGY: Establish terminology to create concepts of oral and nasal sound. Simply say, "Make the sound come out your nose/mouth." Also ask, "Can you hear it coming out of your nose/mouth?"

4. ACCEPT ANY ORAL OR NASAL SOUND: Do not be concerned about the specific oral and nasal sounds the child produces. The oral vocalizations will sound like one or more of the vowels, and the nasal utterances will sound like one or more of the nasal consonants. Do not concern yourself with which of these vowels or nasals the child is making. Make your sole concern whether the child is directing his voice differentially out through the mouth or nose.

5. PRODUCE /ŋ/: Model and encourage the child to say /ŋ/. Some clients at this level of treatment will be able to do so. Respond to this sound in positive ways.

Action Skill 1d

Posturing

Once a child can make sound differentially through the mouth and nose, he learns to position the mouth in basic ways that alter the oral and nasal sounds. In essence, he learns to lower and elevate the jaw, smile, pucker, and round the lips. All of these basic oral positions are achieved in gross fashion. The result of these oral positions is the production of specific early phonemes. When these vocalizations are prolonged, we call it *cooing*.

1. OPEN: The child opens the mouth (lowers the jaw) as he makes an oral sound. A gross production of the vowel /ɑ/ results. This is one of his first true vowels.
2. CLOSE: The child closes the mouth (elevates the jaw) as he makes a nasal sound. A gross production of the nasal consonant /m/ results. This is the child's second consonant.

3. SMILE: The child retracts the lips with the jaw held high as he makes oral sound. A gross production of the vowel /i/ results. This is another first true vowel.

4. PUCKER: The child puckers the lips with the jaw held high as he makes oral sound. A gross production of the vowel /u/ results. This is another first true vowel.

5. ROUND: The child rounds the lips with the jaw somewhat lowered as he makes oral sound. A gross production of vowel /o/ results. This is another first true vowel.

6. CLOSED AT TONGUE: The child closes the mouth by elevating the jaw as he makes a nasal sound. Closure occurs grossly with the body of the tongue. A gross production of the nasal consonant /n/ results. This is the child's third consonant.

Facilitating Basic Oral Postures

The facilitation of oral postures incorporates oral-motor and feeding therapy.

1. CONTINUE: Continue all voice and airflow stimulation activities as described above. The child needs to continue expanding his control of inhalation, exhalation, and voice.

2. JAW MOBILITY: Incorporate oral-motor and feeding techniques that facilitate jaw mobility so that the child can freely move the jaw up and down for the open and closed positions.

3. JAW STABILITY: Incorporate oral-motor and feeding therapy techniques that facilitate

jaw stability so that the child can elevate and clench the jaw. This fixes the jaw in the upward position so that the child can isolate his lip mobility work. Teach him to clench or bite down hard. (Avoid this in cases of temporomandibular joint impairment.)

4. ORAL-MOTOR TECHNIQUES: Incorporate oral-motor therapy techniques that facilitate active lip mobility, especially resistance techniques that encourage rounding, retracting, and puckering.

5. FEEDING TECHNIQUES: Incorporate feeding therapy techniques that facilitate active lip mobility.

6. VOCABULARY: Teach the child to respond correctly to the following commands:

   A. "Close your mouth."
      - Place the lips together for /m/
   B. "Open your mouth."
      - Lower the jaw for /ɑ/
   C. "Smile."
      - Retract the lips for /i/
   D. "Kiss."
      - Pucker the lips for /u/
   E. "Poke out your lips."
      - Round the lips for /o/
   F. "Push your tongue up to the roof of your mouth."
      - Flatten the tongue against the palate for /n/

Stage 2
Speechifying

Making Utterances Sound Speech-like

A CHILD LEARNS TO MAKE HIS UTTERANCES sound like speech during this second stage. He learns to project the voice, alter it into high and low pitch, produce basic intonation patterns, mark syllables by beat, and laugh. All these skills are based upon the child's ability to prolong his voice.

ACTION SKILLS
- projecting
- pitching
- intoning
- pulsing
- laughing

ACTION SKILL 2A
Projecting

Once a child can produce prolonged oral sound his voice begins to change, becoming a little louder and being projected further through the mouth. As such, his first basic vowels become less muffled, more attention getting, and significantly more recognizable. The child's loudest voice will become a shout. Better projection on the nasals make them sound less infantile.

Facilitating Vocal Projection

Vocal projection is encouraged in therapy and during the course of everyday activities.

1. CONTINUE: Continue all voice and airflow stimulation activities as described above.
2. MODELING: Model the loud voice and encourage others to do so.
3. AMPLIFIERS: Vocal projection is best encour-

aged by voicing into natural sound amplifiers. Encourage the child to voice into a variety of toys and tools—vinyl tubes, paper towel tubes, large bowls and pots, stacker cups, PVC plumbing joints, small and large cardboard boxes, plastic toy microphones, real and toy telephones, and funnels.

4. LARGE SPACES: Encourage the child to be loud on the playground. Shout to one another across a large room.

5. CONCEPTS: Teach the child the concepts of *loud voice* and *soft voice*. Teach him to make his voice "fill the whole room" or "fill the whole box."

6. RESTRICT THE LOUD VOICE: You do not want your child to be shouting all the time. Therefore, it is critical that while you are encouraging him to be loud you also disallow a loud voice at specific times. Teach him about the *inside voice* and the *outside voice*. Remove him from situations where he is being too loud—i.e., restaurants, the grocery store, church, and so forth. Teach him about being quiet. Use the signal "shhh." Say, "It is time to be quiet now."

ACTION SKILL 2B
Pitching

A prolonged sound allows a child to begin experimenting with pitch. Most children begin to experiment with pitch in gross ways: by elevating voice up to a squeal and by lowering it down to a growl. A child's attempt to reach up and down in pitch causes him to pass through all the other pitch points in between. The result is a voice that can alter pitch up and down the scale.

Facilitating Pitch Alterations
Pitch alterations are taught in a variety of ways.

1. CONTINUE: Continue all voice and airflow stimulation activities as described above.
2. MODELING: Help children learn to make pitch variations by modeling the extremes. Exaggerate high pitch and low growl.

3. TOYS: Train the ear to hear pitch variations by providing an assortment of horns, whistles, and sirens that present various pitch sounds.

4. NATURAL GESTURES: Use your body to mark high and low pitch. Stretch up high to demonstrate high pitch, and scrunch down low to mark low pitch. Use your arms as well. Raise them to mark high pitch and lower them to mark low pitch.

5. ANIMAL SOUNDS: Develop the child's conceptual framework for pitch by using animal sounds. High-pitch animal sounds include the kitten's mew, the mouse's squeak, the bird's tweet, and the monkey's chatter. Low-pitch animal sounds include the large dog's bark, the cat's purr, and the lion's roar.

Action Skill 2c
Intoning

The ability to prolong sound, project voice, and make pitch variation allow children to intone. This is the ability to alter pitch in speech-like fashion within a single vocalization. The most basic and important of all the intonation patterns in standard North American English is the high-to-low pattern of statements. But also include the low-to-high pattern of questions, and the low-high-low pattern of exaggeration.

Facilitating Intonation Patterns
Intonation patterns are taught through exaggeration and modeling.

1. CONTINUE: Continue all voice and airflow stimulation activities as described above.
2. MODEL: Teach intonation patterns through exaggerated modeling. Prolong single words

and exaggerate phrases and sentences to make the high-low intonation pattern stand out. Present utterances in a singsong manner.

3. GESTURE CUES: Mark the intonation patterns with body and arm movements or facial expressions.

4. ESTABLISH SPECIFIC PATTERNS: Use a specific intonation pattern when producing specific words or phrases. For example, say, "I love you", "Time for bed", and "Let's go!" each with their unique intonation pattern every time.

ACTION SKILL 2D

Pulsing

The first syllable-like markings that appear on prolonged vocalizations result from rhythmic body movements. We will call this *pulsing*. Pulsing arises as a child vocalizes while rocking on hands and knees, bouncing up and down, flexing the trunk, waving the arms, kicking the leg, and bending the knees while standing. Pulsing develops as children learn to move in rhythmic ways.

Facilitating Beat Properties

Pulsing is fun to stimulate because it involves rhythmic body movements.

1. CONTINUE: Continue all voice and airflow stimulation activities as described above.
2. BOUNCING: Vocalize with the child while bouncing him rhythmically on your lap, on a therapy ball, or on a trampoline.

3. HANDS AND KNEES: Encourage the child to vocalize while he is rocking forward and back in crawling position.

4. TRUNK FLEXING: Teach the child to engage in rhythmic, up-and-down trunk movements (trunk flexing) while vocalizing.

5. KICKING THE LEGS: Teach the client to kick his legs while lying in supine. For example, hang a balloon from a string attached to the ceiling. Have the child vocalize while kicking the balloon.

6. ARM FLAPPING: Pretend to fly while vocalizing. Have the arms move up and down rhythmically.

7. MODELING: Teach pulsing through exaggerated modeling. Make big movements yourself.

Action Skill 2e
Laughing

Laughing is not speech. But laughing is an important step in the development of vocalizations because it exercises deep inhalation and extensive sound prolongation. Good, hearty, belly laughing is the longest of the prolonged sounds. It is loud, can be oral or nasal, and is made with wide swings in pitch and intonation. As such, laughter is the most advanced way a child exercises all of the skills he has learned so far. And purposefully laughing is an important milestone in controlled vocal output. It marks the end of the second stage of vocal learning. It is a springboard to the third stage.

Facilitating Laughter
Laughter can be encouraged in as many different ways as there are children who laugh.

1. CONTINUE: Continue all voice and airflow stimulation activities as described above.

2. LAUGH YOURSELF: Real laughter is contagious, so the best way to encourage it is to laugh yourself. Lighten up your therapy room, your classroom, or your home.

3. FIND THE TRIGGER: Children differ by age and personality in the types of things that elicit their laughter. Laughter can be elicited through tickling, chasing, or roughhouse play. Laughter can be elicited in response to funny faces, slapstick antics, or hide-and-seek routines. Laughter often comes in response to words or phrases that are silly, rhyming, or taboo. Sudden and unexpected events can create an atmosphere filled with laughter. Balloons, puppies, and pretending to be a kangaroo can cause lots of laughter. Adults must experiment widely to find that which causes laughter in each child.

4. FREQUENCY: Laughter should be exercised often when children are rounding out their second stage of vocal development.

5. AVOID ASSUMPTIONS ABOUT TICKLING: Don't assume that all children laugh when tickled. Some children hate being tickled and will do everything they can to avoid it.

Stage 3
Honing

Zeroing In on Non-vocalic Consonants
Differentiated by Place

DURING STAGE 3 A CHILD LEARNS to produce a variety of non-vocalic consonants by acquiring five specific action skills. By the end, he is able to produce all the stop and hissing phonemes. These skills also are dependent on the ability to inhale deeply and to prolong vocal production.

ACTION SKILLS
- vibrating
- occluding
- releasing
- popping
- fricating
- vowelizing

ACTION SKILL 3A

Vibrating

A child's ability to prolong exhalation allows him to experiment with the changes that occur as air and voice pass through vocal tract constrictions. Constricting loosely at various points along the vocal tract results in the production of the vibratory sounds we call *raspberries*. A raspberry (RSP) can be both voiced and voiceless, and it can be made in one of several places along the vocal tract. Raspberries lay the groundwork for place of articulation from anterior to posterior. In other words, the ability to produce consonants differently by place from front to back along the vocal tract is discovered as the full array of raspberries is acquired.

Raspberries also lay the foundation for all the stops and hissing sounds. Raspberries stimulate a high level of oral-tactile awareness. They draw a child's attention to his mouth and "wake up" the oral mechanism like never before. We shall label these sounds RSP-1,

RSP-2, and so forth. Readers are strongly urged to try each one as described below.

- RSP-1: a voiceless raspberry made at the lips (bilabial)
- RSP-2: a voiced raspberry made at the lips (bilabial)
- RSP-3: a voiceless raspberry made with the tongue-tip and lips (lingua-labial)
- RSP-4: a voiced raspberry made with the tongue-tip and lips (lingua-labial)
- RSP-5: a voiceless raspberry made at the tongue-back and velum (lingua-velar)
- RSP-6: a voiced raspberry made at the tongue-back and velum (lingua-velar)
- RSP-7: a voiceless raspberry made in the trachea (tracheal)
- RSP-8: a voiced raspberry made in the trachea (tracheal)
- RSP-9: a voiceless raspberry made at the glottis (glottal)
- RSP-10: a voiced raspberry made at the glottis (glottal)
- RSP-11: a raspberry made in the nose (the "snort"; usually ingressive)

Facilitating Vibration

Raspberries result when postures are loosely held during prolonged exhalation and voice.

1. CONTINUE: Continue all voice and airflow stimulation activities as described above.

Concentrate on increasing depth of inhalation and length of prolongation. Prolonged exhalation is critical for raspberry production. You should see a significant increase in these skills during the time period in which the raspberries emerge.

2. RASPBERRY BLOWER: There is one blow toy that gives children the concept of blowing raspberries before they are able to do so. A raspberry blower has a small mouthpiece with a balloon-like tube on the end. When a child blows through the mouthpiece, the rubber tube vibrates and makes a sound just like a raspberry. This gives a child the vibrotactile feel of a raspberry, an idea that encourages him to make one with his own mouth. When the child moves into this stage, have him practice with the raspberry blower frequently.

3. JAW STABILITY: A high jaw position is critical for the bilabial, lingua-labial, and lingua-velar raspberries to emerge because its high position allows the articulators to articulate. With a high jaw position, the upper and lower lips can meet, the tongue-tip can slip between the lips, and the back of the tongue can reach the velum. Therefore, techniques to get the jaw high are in order. Work on increasing strength of the bite and chew, and strengthen the masseters. Help the child learn to pull the jaw up (close the mouth). If low tone is the reason for the low-slung jaw position, increase overall strength of the oral musculature.

4. EXPERIMENT WITH PLACE: Most children develop one of the raspberries and use it for a while before the others emerge. Allow the child to play with this first vibratory sound as often as he wants to strengthen it. Make it automatic. Then use it to introduce the others. Encourage the child to make raspberry sounds in all the other places of articulation.

5. MODELS: Make sure to model all these sounds yourself.

6. VISUAL, TACTILE, AND AUDITORY CUES: Show the child what to do, give tactile stimulation to the mouth specifically by place, and make sure these sounds stand out audibly through slight amplification and repetition.

7. FEEDING THERAPY: Most children acquire raspberries while eating pureed food, i.e., they produce raspberries to blow out food they don't want. This can be used as a therapy method under the right circumstances.

8. SPITTING: Many children learn to produce raspberries while spitting. While this is an undesirable behavior, it can be useful for a short period of time. Tell him, "No spitting," and wipe his mouth briskly with a paper or cloth towel. Teach him to spit out when appropriate.

9. ASSIGN MEANING: Make each raspberry stand out by assigning a meaning to it.
   - Bilabial raspberries can be used for motor sounds.
   - Lingua-labial raspberries can be used to indicate rejection.

- Lingua-velar raspberries can be used for crashing sounds.
- Tracheal raspberries can be used for animal growls.
- Glottal raspberries can be used to represent the scary noises of monsters.

10. LABEL PLACE OF ARTICULATION: As the raspberries appear, build a vocabulary for place of articulation. Talk about where the raspberries are made with phrases:
    - "with your lips"
    - "with your tongue"
    - "in the back of your mouth"
    - "in your throat"

ACTION SKILL 3B
Occluding

Once a child can produce raspberries he begins to add more tension to these productions. The result is a complete occlusion of the air stream at the lips, tongue-tip, tongue-back, and glottis. The child is learning to stop airflow in each place of articulation. Most children experiment with this tension, alternately building from a raspberry to the occluded position, and the releasing from the occluded position back into the raspberry. When the child finally does learn to release each occluded position with a burst, the productions will turn into true plosive consonants.

Facilitating Occlusion

Occlusion occurs as the result of significantly increased tension applied to oral position.

1. CONTINUE: Continue all voice and airflow stimulation activities as described above.

2. CONTINUE RASPBERRY TECHNIQUES: Since the occluded positions are the direct result of experimentation with the raspberries, all the methods for stimulating the raspberries should continue.

3. INCREASE ORAL TENSION: Occlusion results when the articulators press together more firmly. Incorporate techniques to increase the strength of lips and tongue.

4. JAW STABILITY: Occluded sounds evolve when the jaw can be held high for extended periods. Incorporate techniques to increase masseter strength.

5. MECHANICAL OCCLUSION: The concept of occluding airflow can be taught by occluding the mouth with a large object that is soft but that can be pressed firmly against the mouth—i.e., a hand, stuffed toy, pillow, or blanket. Press the object firmly but safely against the mouth while the child is vocalizing. The outside pressure will occlude the stream of sound.

Action Skill 3c

Releasing

Once a child can occlude in all the positions described above, he learns to release his firm closures with a small burst of voice. The release is accomplished by quickly lowering the jaw after pressure is built. The result is the child's first gross production of CV syllables with voiced stop consonants. Neutral vowels are used when these skills first appear. With time, these neutral vowels become the vowels he learned earlier: /i/, /u/, /ɑ/, and /o/.

- /b/+vowel results when bilabial occlusion is released into a vowel
- /d/+vowel results when lingua-labial occlusion is released into a vowel
- /g/+vowel results when lingua-velar occlusion is released into a vowel
- /ʔ/+vowel results when glottal occlusion is released into a vowel

Releasing skill quickly transfers to CV utterances with the other consonants he has learned: /m/, /n/, and /ŋ/. This calls for celebration! With releasing skills, a child can begin to produce his first real words and phrases made of both consonants and vowels. This basic CV pattern is the cornerstone of all his word and phrase learning from this point forward.

CV Words

With the CV releasing skill, a child can say a variety of words that have the basic CV construction.

- /b/ – boo, bee, B, bow, buh
- /d/ – do, dough, Dee, day, duh
- /g/ – goo, go, gay, guh
- /m/ – me, May, moo, mow, ma (mom)
- /n/ – knee, nay, new, no

Other Simple Words

The CV construction also allows the child to say other simple words by forcing the words into the basic CV pattern. This allows him to say more words than he otherwise could. Consider the following:

- *car* pronounced /kɑ/
- *boat* pronounced /bo/
- *sheep* pronounced /di/
- *that* pronounced /dæ/
- *song* pronounced /ŋɔ/
- *float* pronounced /do/

Complex Words

The CV releasing pattern also allows a child to say complex words and phrases in a CV pattern.

- *pencil* pronounced /bɛ/
- *polar bear* pronounced /bɛ/
- *sugar cookies* pronounced /gu/
- *Doctor David* pronounced /de/
- *storybook* pronounced /dɑ/

Facilitating Release Actions

Release actions are accomplished by lowering the jaw quickly after occlusion is accomplished and pressure built.

1. CONTINUE: Continue all voice and airflow stimulation activities as described above.
2. OCCLUSION: Make sure your client is producing the voiced raspberries and has begun to occlude them.
3. JAW LOWERING: Incorporate techniques to mobilize the jaw. Get it to move up and down.
4. OBJECTS: Teach the concept of building up inter-oral air pressure by using the hand or another object pressed against the mouth while vocalizing. Use the object to stop vocalization, and use a quick release of the object to teach plosiveness.
5. GLOTTAL RELEASE: Glottal occlusion is released into a vowel without assistance from the jaw. It is released simply by opening the glottis. It

is usually learned with heavy lifting and exaggerated effort.

Focusing on Words

Once a child is producing words, we begin to add techniques from traditional articulation therapy. These techniques will be referred to throughout the subsequent stages of phoneme development. Basic techniques to be used whenever we are stimulating words are described as follows.

1. LISTEN: Open your ears to your child's spontaneous utterances. Listen *for* and *to* them. Determine which syllable patterns are present. Accept utterances for which you find yourself thinking, *I think he said* . . . . He probably did say that word or phrase.

2. ASSIGN MEANING: Assign meaning to those things you hear your child say. If he spontaneously says "bah", give it a meaning, such as *bye, baby, bottle,* or *blanket.* The child may use this utterance to mean that item for a while.

3. EXPECT GENERALIZATION OF MEANING: Realize that utterances that sound like specific words may change meaning. For example, the child may use "dada" to mean *daddy.* After a while, he may use this utterance to mean every male he encounters. Then he may use it to name everything in the room. This is normal. Your child is *generalizing.* After a period of generalization, he will return the utterance to the original meaning.

4. ECHO: Repeat words and phrases back to the child exactly the way he said them. If he calls the dog "goggie", then you do the same. This *baby talk* will not harm him. Instead, echoing a child's utterance will teach him what he is saying. It will help him reflect upon his own utterances. It will teach him to hear himself.

5. ECHO CORRECTION: Echo back your child's words and phrases with correct articulation. When he calls the dog "goggie", repeat back "doggie." This allows him to hear the correct way the word is pronounced.

6. MODEL: Speak simple words and phrases clearly. Don't add any other comments to the model. This will confuse him. Simply model exactly what you want him to say.

7. ENCOURAGE FREQUENT USE: Any word that has made its appearance should be encouraged often. Make up excuses to practice new words. For example, if he says /dɔ/ for "dog", then talk about the dog several times per day. Name "dog" when petting and feeding the dog, when looking at a picture book that depicts a dog, when telling daddy about walking the dog, and so forth.

8. CREATE A SPEECH BOOK: An old-fashioned technique that is quite useful throughout all stages of phoneme learning is the speech book. Draw simple pictures of the words your child can say. Have him help you or draw the pictures himself. Label the word with big block letters. Place the picture in a three-ring binder. Add a new picture for each

word learned. Use the speech book like other picture books. Encourage your child to name the pictures using his new words. This allows him to practice these words with you and other family members, friends, therapists, and teachers.

9. TRAIN OTHERS TO HEAR WHAT YOU HEAR: Make sure that everyone who communicates with the child knows what words to expect from him. Make sure they can recognize these words when your child says them. For example, say, "When he says 'ba', that means *up*."

10. USE VISUAL FEEDBACK: Encourage the child to watch himself in a mirror as he is saying words. This gives him visual input about his oral movements.

11. USE AMPLIFICATION: Amplify the child's own voice slightly by speaking into tubes, funnels, microphones, etc. This will make his own words stand out.

12. DRILL AND DRILL PLAY: Encourage the child to say his new word many times in a row. Tell him, "Say it again." Or echo his word back and expect him to say it. Apraxic children need to rehearse words often.

13. PLAY WITH WORDS: Have fun and make fun while saying new words. Say them while marching, hopping, and bouncing. Say them while shouting, calling, and whispering. Repeat them every time you point to a picture of the word, and point ten times in a row. Repeat the word while putting toys away. Say the word with each toy that is tossed in the toy box.

14. WORK IN CYCLES: Practice one word many times a day for several days and then drop it. Pick up a new word and make that the target for several days. Then drop it too. Continue with new words every day or every few days. Return to old words that have been dropped and stimulate them again for a few days.

15. EXAGGERATE WORDS: Make the words you model stand out in some specific way. Use a sign signal, make a silly gesture, or use exaggerated facial expressions when saying a word.

16. RHYME: Say simple words in rhymes. For example, have fun saying "do, goo, boo, moo!"

17. BOMBARD: Say a target word several times during a quiet time. For example, as the child watches bees moving from flower to flower in your yard, say, "Bee . . . bee . . . bee . . . bee."

18. ORIENT THE CHILD TO YOUR FACE: Place your hands near your face, cup your hands around your mouth, or cup your hands around your whole face as you say words.

19. OTHER ARTICULATION AND PHONOLOGICAL METHODS: All other traditional articulation and phonological methods fit neatly into therapy when working at the word level.

Action Skill 3d
Popping

Occluded positions also are released voicelessly to create phonemes /p/, /t/, and /k/. At first, these sounds are produced with little air movement, even ingressive air movement. That is why the action skill is called *popping*. Over time a child learns to build up inter-oral air pressure and push more air through the mouth. Then he produces actual voiceless stop consonants as a result.

1. /p/ results when bilabial occlusion is released voicelessly
2. /t/ results when lingua-labial occlusion is released voicelessly
3. /k/ results when lingua-velar occlusion is released voicelessly
4. /ʔ/ results when glottal occlusion is released voicelessly

Facilitating Popping Sounds

Popping sounds are accomplished by lowering the jaw quickly after occlusion has been accomplished and pressure built. This is done without voice.

1. CONTINUE: Continue all voice and airflow stimulation activities as described above.

2. OCCLUSION: Make sure your client is producing the voiceless raspberries and has begun to occlude them.

3. JAW LOWERING: Incorporate techniques to mobilize the jaw. Get it to move up and down.

4. OBJECTS: Teach the concept of building up inter-oral air pressure by using the hand or another object pressed against the mouth while moving air. Use the object to stop vocalization, and use a quick release of the object to teach plosiveness.

5. GLOTTAL RELEASE: Glottal occlusion is released without assistance from the jaw. It is released simply by opening the glottis. It is usually learned with heavy lifting and exaggerated effort.

ACTION SKILL 3E

Fricating

Frication is discovered as children learn to refine the gross vibratory productions of the voiced and voiceless raspberries. Clumsy productions of /f/, /v/, /θ/, /ð/, /s/, /z/, /ʃ/, /ʒ/, /tʃ/, /dʒ/, and /h/ are the result. These sounds are produced in isolation, not in syllables. The phonemes themselves are unstable by place. They are not "locked in."

1. /f/ results from fricating voicelessly between the lower lip and upper teeth
2. /v/ results from fricating with voice between the lower lip and upper teeth
3. /θ/ results from fricating voicelessly between the tongue and upper teeth
4. /ð/ results from fricating with voice between the tongue and upper teeth
5. /s/ results from fricating voicelessly between the tongue and alveolar ridge

6. /z/ results from fricating with voice between the tongue and alveolar ridge
7. /ʃ/ results from fricating voicelessly between the tongue and palate
8. /ʒ/ results from fricating with voice between the tongue and palate
9. /tʃ/ results from stopping and fricating voicelessly between the tongue and palate
10. /dʒ/ results from stopping and fricating with voice between the tongue and palate
11. /h/ results from fricating slightly and voicelessly at the glottis

Facilitating Frication

The hissing phonemes are best learned by making them salient.

1. CONTINUE: Continue all voice and airflow stimulation activities as described above.
2. MODEL: Model the hissing sounds clearly and distinctly so the child can hear them.
3. AMPLIFICATION: Make these quiet hissing sounds louder with amplification through tubes, funnels, or megaphones.
4. MEANING: Assign each phoneme a meaning.
   - /f/: the sound of a cat's wrath
   - /v/: the sound of a speedboat motor
   - /s/: the sound of a snake's hiss
   - /z/: the sound of a buzzing bee
   - /ʃ/: the sound meaning *be quiet.*
   - /ʒ/: the sound of an airplane motor
   - /tʃ/: the "choo-choo" sound of an old train

- /dʒ/: the sound of jumping
- /h/: the sound of being satisfied, worn out, or completed

ACTION SKILL 3F

Vowelizing

Vowelizing is another new term. It refers to a child's production of a very long vowel sound that is purposefully twisted and bent to make a variety of other vowel sounds in slow, continuous sequences. When a child vowelizes, he begins with one vowel. While prolonging that vowel, the child bends it so that it transitions into another vowel. From this second vowel, the child continues prolongation and changes oral shape into a third vowel, and so forth. The child is playing and experimenting with his ability to change the acoustic parameters of sound by making subtle oral-position adjustments to prolonged vowel productions. A child might say, "Ahhhhhheeeeohhhuhhhhwwwoo ooo." He might do this while singing or while simply playing quietly alone or in the company of others.

Vowelizing is done primarily for pleasure and self-entertainment, but important speech skills are learned in the process. Vowelizing helps tune the ear to subtle variations in vowel sound. Through this work the child will learn to produce any vowels he has not yet learned.

Encouraging Vowelizing

We return to our respiration and phonation toys when we facilitate vowelizing.

1. BREATH CONTROL: Vowelizing is encouraged as inhalation gets deeper and as exhalation is prolonged. Include activities to improve trunk support as well as more difficult blow-toy work.

2. SPEECH RESPONSE TOYS: Encourage the child to vocalize longer in order to keep the speech response toys active longer.

3. TUBES: To encourage prolonged vowel sound production use the long flexible tubes—one end at the child's mouth and the other at the child's ear. Encourage the child to bite down and then release the tube in order to change oral position. Encourage him to alter lip position around the tube to change the oral shape and resultant vowel sound.

4. SONGS: Certain songs encourage vowelizing. Consider the refrain *e-i-e-i-o* in "Old McDonald." Any song can be sung with vowels only.

5. COUNTING: Count aloud using only the vowel sounds. Kids usually like this because it allows them to count for a long time before they know the names of all the numbers.

6. ALPHABET: Recite the alphabet using only the vowel sounds.

Stage 4
Oscillating

Creating Primitive Sequences
With Reciprocating Oral Movements

A CHILD BEGINS TO BABBLE during stage 4. Babbling requires extensive prolongation of sound that can be marked by rhythmic back-and-forth (oscillating) oral movements. This process begins with isolated gross movements of the jaw and extends to specific lip and tongue oscillations. All these movements begin haltingly and arrhythmically, and end rhythmic and bouncy.

ACTION SKILLS
- jaw babbling
- silent sequencing
- lip babbling
- tongue babbling
- classic babbling
- advanced babbling

ACTION SKILL 4A
Jaw Babbling

Oscillation begins with gross up-and-down jaw movements as a child prolongs one of the vocalic sounds he has learned so far. A huge number of specific new vocal patterns emerge. These have been given names that correspond to their actions.

1. *mahing.* The sound that results when a child produces /m/ and then moves the jaw up and down. When the jaw lowers, /m/ changes to /ɑ/.
2. *emming.* The sound that results when a child maintains lip closure on /m/ as he moves the jaw up and down. Kids learn this while eating.
3. *nahing.* The sound that results when a child produces /n/ and then moves the jaw up and down. When the jaw lowers, /n/ changes to /ɑ/.
4. *enning.* The sound that results when a child maintains tongue-to-palate or tongue-to-lip

contact on /n/ as he moves the jaw up and down. Kids also learn this while eating.

5. *ngahing*. The sound that results when a child produces /ŋ/ and then moves the jaw up and down. When the jaw lowers, /ŋ/ changes to /ɑ/.

6. *enging*. The sound that results when a child maintains tongue-to-velum contact on /ŋ/ as he moves the jaw up and down. Kids also learn this while eating.

7. *numming*. The sound that results when a child lowers the jaw out of /n/ and elevates the jaw to /m/. Kids learn this while eating.

8. *ngumming*. The sound that results when a child lowers the jaw out of /ŋ/ and elevates the jaw to /m/. Kids learn this while eating.

9. *ah-ing*. The sound that results when a child maintains /ɑ/ and then moves the jaw up and down. A nonspecific glide emerges in the process.

10. *oo-ing*. The sound that results when a child maintains /u/ and then moves the jaw up and down. Primitive /w/ emerges in the process.

11. *ee-ing*. The sound that results when a child maintains /i/ and then moves the jaw up and down. Primitive /y/ emerges in the process.

12. *oh-ing*. The sound that results when a child maintains /o/ and then moves the jaw up and down. Another occurrence of primitive /w/ emerges in the process.

13. *ai-ing*. The sound that results when a child attains /ɑ/ and then moves the jaw up and down. The tongue retracts and elevates in the back when the jaw is high. Primitive /y/ and /ɑi/ emerge in the process.

14. *uh-ing*. Results when the child maintains /ʌ/ and then moves the jaw up and down. A non-specific glide emerges in the process.

15. *lalling*. The sound that results when a child protrudes the tongue between the lips and moves the jaw up and down while vocalizing a non-specific sound. Very primitive /l/ results.

16. *lateral lalling*. The sound that results when a child moves the jaw left and right while vocalizing a nonspecific sound. The tongue usually protrudes somewhat. This is the only sound produced with lateral instead of medial jaw movement. It indicates complete differentiation of jaw from head movements.

Facilitating Jaw Babbling

Jaw babbling is all about getting the jaw to move up and down.

1. CONTINUE: Continue all voice and airflow stimulation activities as described above. Another significant increase in airflow capacity is needed for babbling to emerge.

2. JAW MOVEMENT: Get the jaw to move up and down. That is the key to jaw babbling. Use oral-motor and feeding techniques.

3. ORAL POSTURES: Continue to establish the specific oral postures learned in action skill 1d: "Posturing." Distinct jaw babbling sequences are possible only when basic oral postures are excellent. Distorted basic sounds will result in distorted jaw babbling sequences and, eventually, distorted word productions.

ACTION SKILL 4B

Silent Sequencing

Oscillating movements also are practiced with all the voiceless sounds. A mixture of ingressive and eggressive air movement is noted during production of these voiceless sequences, with the result being more panting, rather than producing an individual phoneme in isolation and then repeating it. Outward moving air begins to dominate as oscillation and respiratory skills advance. We might call this silent sequencing *pre-whispering*.

Silent sequencing is accomplished through discoveries about airflow. Some are made with big up-and-down jaw movements. Some are made with the jaw high. And one is made with the jaw low.

1. BIG UP-AND-DOWN JAW MOVEMENTS: The voiceless stops—/p/, /t/, /k/—and the voiceless hissing sounds—/f/, /θ/, /s/, /ʃ/, /tʃ/—are rehearsed in sequence by moving the jaw

up and down in gross fashion. These big jaw movements are the same ones used in "Jaw Babbling" above.

2. JAW HELD HIGH: The hissing sounds—/f/, /θ/, /s/, /ʃ/, /tʃ/—are also made with a stable high jaw position. As the jaw is held high, the child hits and holds one of these oral positions and then pants through them. All six of these hissing phonemes are produced grossly during this period. Much distortion and overlap of sounds is heard. Some movement of the tongue is noted to achieve the child's /tʃ/-like sounds.

3. JAW HELD LOW: Phoneme /h/ is made with the jaw held low. This is true panting.

4. JAW ELEVATED/MOUTH CLOSED: Sniffing is produced with the mouth closed.

Each action results in the production of a specific vocalization, and these have been named according to the phoneme produced. These designations result in a few unfortunate names. Please forgive these titles by keeping the purpose of our discussion in mind.

1. *pee-ing.* The silent sequencing of /p/
2. *tee-ing.* The silent sequencing of /t/
3. *kay-ing.* The silent sequencing of /k/
4. *eff-ing.* The silent sequencing of /f/
5. *eth-ing.* The silent sequencing of /θ/
6. *ess-ing.* The silent sequencing of /s/
7. *esh-ing.* The silent sequencing of /ʃ/
8. *etch-ing.* The silent sequencing of /tʃ/
9. *panting.* The silent sequencing of /h/

10. *sniffing.* The silent sequencing of nasal sound made while the mouth is closed

11. *primitive blowing.* The silent sequencing of voiceless sound made with the mouth open and the lips slightly rounded

Facilitating Silent Sequencing

There are two main aspects to the development of silent sequencing. The first is up-and-down jaw movement. The second is sequential production of exhaled air.

1. CONTINUE: Continue all voice and airflow stimulation activities as described above.

2. JAW MOVEMENT: Get the jaw to move up and down. That is the first key to silent sequencing. Use oral-motor and feeding techniques.

3. PANTING: Get the child to pant; that is, to inhale and exhale in short, rapid sequences. That is another key to establishing silent sequences. Panting is done with /h/. Then transfer the panting skill to the other hissing sounds. Keep in mind that your child may learn to pant in one of the other hissing positions.

4. ORAL POSTURES: Continue to establish the specific oral postures learned in action skill 1d: "Posturing" above. Distinct silent sequences are possible only when basic oral postures are excellent. Distorted basic sounds will result in distorted jaw babbling sequences.

ACTION SKILL 4C
Lip Babbling

Children also oscillate lip movements while pro-longing sound. These basic lip movements are made while the jaw is held high and lightly clenched. Two new patterns emerge.

1. *Oo-ee-ing* results when the lips pucker and retract in sequence
2. *Woo-ing* results when the lips pucker and release in sequence

Facilitating Lip Babbling

Lip Babbling will occur when the lips are active while the jaw is stable.

1. CONTINUE: Continue all voice and airflow stimulation activities as described above.
2. ACTIVATE THE LIPS: Employ oral-motor and feeding techniques to activate the lips. Get

them to pucker, round, and retract more
often and with greater skill.

3. ELEVATE THE JAW: Employ oral-motor and
   feeding techniques to elevate the jaw. Get it
   high and strong. Teach the client to clench.

ACTION SKILL 4D

Tongue Babbling

Oscillating movements of the tongue cause primitive babbling sequences while the mouth is open—i.e., the jaw is lowered—and sound is prolonged. This is the first time the child actively tries to differentiate his tongue movements from his jaw movements in order to deliver speech-like utterances. Voiceless trials sneak in on occasion. However, true tongue babbling is voiced. The specific vocalizations that result are named for the acoustic quality they achieve.

1. *blubbling*. The sound that results when the tongue tip moves in and out between the lips that are slightly parted. This is often the very first tongue movement vocalization. Tip movements are weak, asymmetrical, clumsy, and arrhythmic. The jaw is essentially inactive but positioned just low enough to allow the tongue tip to slip forward and back.

2. *blalling*. The sound that results when the tongue becomes much more active. The jaw is positioned low. From the neutral position inside the mouth, the tongue protrudes out and down toward the chin. Then it pulls back into the mouth. During the process, the tongue tip brushes forward and back against the upper lip, the upper teeth, and the alveolar ridge. A primitive /l/ results.

3. *dlelling*. The sound that results when the tongue oscillates back and forward at the alveolar ridge and upper lip. The tip elevates somewhat. Primitive /l/ with true tip elevation results. Dlelling often emerges as the child explores his newly-erupted upper incisors.

4. *lerring*. The sound that results when the tongue oscillates back and forward inside the mouth while the jaw is lowered somewhat. From neutral, the tongue curls up and back toward the velum. Then it moves back down to neutral again. A primitive retroflex /r/ results as the tongue curls up and back toward the velum.

5. *blerring*. The sound that results when a child combines blalling and lerring. The tongue stretches out and down toward the chin, and then curls up and back toward the velum. Rehearsal of primitive /l/ and /r/ sequences results.

6. *lateral lerring*. The sound that results when the tongue moves left and right while the jaw remains stable at mid line. Lateral lerring is done both inside and outside the mouth. Several non-speech sounds result. Although

this specific vocalization does not lend itself directly to a mature phoneme, this lateral motion during sound production is a critical step in vocal development. It indicates complete differentiation of tongue movements from jaw movements.

Facilitating Tongue Babbling

The key to tongue babbling is to get the tongue to move independently from the jaw while the child is vocalizing.

1. CONTINUE: Continue all voice and airflow stimulation activities as described above.
2. JAW STABILITY: Now we want to train the child to open his mouth wide and to hold the jaw low.
3. TONGUE MOBILITY: Employ oral-motor and feeding techniques to activate the tongue. Get it to move out and in, forward and back, and left and right.
4. VOCABULARY: Establish one label to describe each action. For example,
   a. "Poke your tongue in and out"
   b. "Make your tongue stick out as far as you can"
   c. "Make your tongue go over here. . . . Then over here"
   d. "Curl your tongue way up in the back"
5. MOVING THE TONGUE WITHOUT VOICE: Some children cannot vocalize while moving the tongue. Teach them to move the tongue silently at first. Then add voice as skill improves.

ACTION SKILL 4E

Classic Babbling

Classic babbling is the oscillation pattern with which we are all familiar. Classic babbling is the sequential production of consonants (C) and vowels (V) in well-defined repeating syllables. The designation "CV CV CV" will be used.

Classic babbling, as defined here, incorporates a limited list of phonemes. That list includes:

- The three nasals—/m/, /n/, /ŋ/
- The four glides—/w/, /l/, /y/, /r/
- The three voiced stops —/b/, /d/, /g/
- Five basic vowels /ɑ/, /i/, /u/, /o/, /ʌ/

Other phonemes slip in on occasion. For our purposes, classic babbling is limited to these fifteen phonemes. Children produce every possible combination of these consonants and vowels while babbling in a classic way. We note simple sequences like /bɑ bɑ bɑ/ as well as very difficult ones like /ɚ ɚ ɚ/.

Classic babbling is a child's way of rehearsing identical syllables in repetitious drills. Such rehearsal solidifies both the phonemes and the CV syllables produced. This gives him the firm foundation of sound production he needs to carry him into production of real words—a skill that is just around the corner.

Classic babbling and respiratory control enjoy a reciprocal relationship. The strings elongate as respiratory control improves, and respiratory control improves as classic babbling strings lengthen.

Classic babbling is devoid of the intonation and stress patterns associated with jargon, so it does not sound like speech, *per se*. It sounds like babbling. Children quickly discover that this is an amusing way to capture an audience. Family members and other adults usually pay attention to these sounds and happily join in their production. Babbling sequences often are the first sounds family members recognize as speech-like.

Facilitating Classic Babbling

Classic babbling will emerge once all the prior action skills converge.

1. CONTINUE: Every technique named so far should be continued.
2. MODEL: Model sequences for the child to hear and see.
3. BABY PLAY: Pretending to be babies is an excellent way to practice classic babbling sequences. Children who begrudge that babbling is a "baby" thing to do may need to pretend to be babies in order to feel comfortable

doing it. Or they can pretend that a baby doll is making the sounds.

4. CHALLENGES: Some children do not want to pretend to be babies, do not want to play with baby dolls, and definitely do not want to babble. However, they often can be challenged. Say, "I bet you can't say . . ." Then, after he produces the babbling sequence, act astonished by saying, "I didn't know you could say that!" This often does the trick.

5. FORBIDDEN BABBLING: Another way to persuade a stubborn child is to tell him *not* to babble. With a gleam in your eye, tell him, "Don't say . . . ." When he produces the babbling sequence for you, act upset by saying, "Hey! I told you not to say . . . ." Then he will probably say it again. Continue this banter so that the child rehearses the sequence several times in a row. Then switch to another sequence. Forbidden practice will work until the child figures out the game. Until then, it is a verbal game in which he will engage regularly.

6. ALPHABET SOUNDS: Another way to encourage classic babbling is to incorporate the ABCs and the sounds they make. Practice saying /mɑ mɑ mɑ/ for the sound of *m*, /wʌ wʌ wʌ/ for the sound of *w*, and so forth.

7. PUPPETS: Puppets can be named and given a specific sound to rehearse babbling sequences. For example, a frog puppet can say, "Guh guh guh."

ACTION SKILL 4F
Advanced Babbling

We will use the term *advanced babbling* to refer to babbling that incorporates the voiceless stops—/p/, /t/, /k/—as well as the voiceless and voiced hissing sounds—/f/, /v/, /θ/, /ð/, /s/, /z/, /ʃ/, /ʒ/, /tʃ/, /dʒ/, and /h/. This is so advanced that the average child learning speech at a normal rate does not engage in its production until some time after real words are produced. And many children do not rehearse it at all. Have you ever heard a little baby babble /si si si/ or /vei vei vei/? Probably not. By the time most kids can produce these types of sounds in sequences they are already at the word level. But advanced babbling is included here because children with apraxia or dysarthria often need to spend some time learning these patterns. Like classic babbling, advanced babbling also is void of the intonation and stress patterns of jargon.

Facilitating Advanced Babbling

Continue all procedures for classic babbling above. Incorporate the new set of sounds.

Stage 5
Solidifying

Establishing Basic Syllable Constructions

BY THE END OF STAGE 5, a child will be able to produce protowords, words, protophrases, and phrases with a greater variety of basic syllable shapes, including VCV, VC, CVCV, and VV. These patterns are constructed with all the consonants and vowels learned to date. A child can attempt to say words and phrases with these first basic syllable constructions at the ready.

ACTION SKILLS
- embedding
- closing
- duplicating
- diminutizing
- diphthongizing
- shortening

ACTION SKILL 5A
Embedding

Embedding is the process of placing a consonant sound between two vowel sounds. The result is a VCV pattern. Children produce protowords and words with this simple construction. It is quite common to be one of the first of the word and phrase constructions to emerge. Children freely substitute one consonant for another in making these syllables.

Words

Embedding, or VCV construction, allows a child to produce a huge variety of words. Consider the following examples:

- *all done* produced as /ɔ dʌ/
- *all gone* produced /ɔ gɔ/
- *yogurt* produced as /o yo/
- *sandwich* produced as /æ mi/

- *elephant* produced as /e ʈe/
- *another* produced as /ʌ ŋʌ/

Phrases

Children also produce simple protophrases with the VCV pattern and appropriate intonation and stress. For example:

- *What's that?* produced as /ʌ dæ/
- *I want that* produced as /ʌ dæ/
- *I don't want that* produced as /ʌ dæ/
- *Where are you?* produced as /ɑ du/
- *Where did it go?* produced as /ɛ do/
- *I love you* produced as /ʌ yu/

Facilitating Embedding

Incorporate all techniques described in Focusing on Words in action skill 3c: "Releasing."

ACTION SKILL 5B
Closing

Closing a syllable results in the VC construction. The consonants used in these syllables usually are voiceless stops—/p/, /t/, /k/—voiceless hissing sounds—/f/, /θ/, /s/, /ʃ/, /tʃ/—or voiced nasals—/m/, /n/, /ŋ/.

VC Words

We note this simple VC pattern quite frequently in samples of children's first word productions. For example, words like *up*, *eat*, *out*, *ick!*, *on*, and *off*. These exemplify correctly articulated words. They are made with a correct VC sequence.

Other Simple Words

The VC pattern also is used for simple, one-syllable words that the child is ready to say but cannot produce with an initial consonant. For example:

- *hat* produced as /æt/
- *fish* produced as /ɪʃ/
- *car* produced as /ɑɚ/
- *that* produced as /æt/
- *this* produced as /ɪs/
- *please* produced as /ɪz/

Complex Words

The simple VC pattern is used as a major simplification of much more complex words and phrases. The vowel usually is quite prolonged (designated by /•/) to hold the space for the rest of the word or phrase. Consider the following:

- *elephant* produced as /ɛ•n/
- *garbage* produced as /ɑ•dʒ/
- *Mrs. Carmath* produced /ɑ•ʃ/
- *Doggie wants to go out* produced as /ɑ••t/

Facilitating Closing

Incorporate all techniques described in Focusing on Words in action skill 3c "Releasing."

ACTION SKILL 5C
Duplicating

Duplicating is one of the most common ways children produce early words. It is the production of two identical syllables in sequence as a pattern for a single word. We write this pattern as CVCV, a shortening of the basic classic babbling process.

Universal Words

The CVCV pattern is used the world over for children's early words, such as *mama*, *dada*, *nana*, and *papa* for mother, father, grandmother, and grandfather.

All Words

Children at this stage often fit every single word into the CVCV construction. Consider the following more complex words pushed into the CVCV pattern.

- *peanut butter* pronounced /bʌ bʌ/
- *banana* pronounced /næ næ/
- *Blue's Clues* pronounced /bu bu/
- *Minnie Mouse* pronounced /mi mi/
- *scissors* pronounced /dɪ dɪ/
- *flowers* pronounced /fʌ fʌ/

Duplicating is a child's most powerful tool for saying words and phrases for which he is not otherwise prepared. He can pronounce almost anything in CVCV patterning and the people around him will understand what he is saying if they have a context or a referent for the word. As such, a little toddler can go in the kitchen and announce "buh-buh" and his parents will recognize immediately that he wants a peanut butter and jelly sandwich. Spoken outside the kitchen or to an unfamiliar listener, it will result in a non-successful communication. But armed with dozens of such words, a young child can make his observations and desires known to all who spend time with him and who care to listen.

Facilitating Duplicating

Incorporate all techniques described in Focusing on Words in action skill 3c "Releasing."

ACTION SKILL 5D
Diminutizing

The term *diminutizing* refers to the action of creating diminutive words. Diminutive words are two-syllable constructions that end in *y* or *ie*. For example, we are all familiar with the common diminutives *kitty*, *doggie*, *horsie*, and *birdie*. The *y* or *ie* ending creates a small or diminutive form of the mature words *cat*, *dog*, *horse*, and *bird*.

Diminutized words are easy for children to produce. Diminutizing allows children to produce more words than they are capable. Diminutizing should not be shunned as an inferior form of baby talk. The ability to diminutize is an important stage of expressive speech development. It represents the first time a child produces two syllables in sequence with two different vowels.

Common Words

Some diminutized words are so widespread that they are considered real, whole words. Consider *mommy*, *daddy*, *baby*, and *puppy*. These may have stemmed originally from *mom*, *dad*, *babe*, and *pup*, but at this point in the history of our language it doesn't matter any more. Everyone says "mommy", "daddy", "baby", and "puppy", and your child should too.

Uncommon Diminutives

Children learning to diminutize will go to vast extents to produce words in a diminutized form. For example, a child might call his socks "sockies" and his shoes "shoesies." Unusual forms should be encouraged when the child is learning to diminutize, even though awkward words could result. Try not to cringe when the child wants to call your sedan a "car-y." Play with these new word forms.

Facilitating Diminutizing

Incorporate all techniques described in Focusing on Words in action skill 3c: "Releasing."

ACTION SKILL 5E

Diphthongizing

Diphthongizing is another new form of an old word. A diphthong is a vowel constructed of two vowels and the gliding sounds made between them. We have five diphthongs in English: /au/, /ai/, /ou/, /ei/ and /ɔi/. The following are samples:

- /au/—how
- /ai/—high
- /ou/—hoe
- /ei/—hay
- /ɔi/—ahoy

A slow and careful pronunciation of each of these words should reveal to the reader that each vowel sound actually is constructed of two vowel sounds sequenced together. The vowel of *how* is constructed of /a/ and /u/ in sequence. Diphthongizing is the process of learning to make these two vowels into one new construction. We will designate this pattern as VV.

Diphthongs enhance expressive speech in several ways. First, the inclusion of diphthongs makes a child's speech sound melodious. Without them a child's speech sounds choppy or clipped. Second, diphthongs stretch the production of words in ways that allow time for correct intonation and stress patterns. A lack of diphthongs causes a lack of the stress and intonation patterns. This interferes with intelligibility. Third, lack of diphthongs also causes a shortening of words. This inhibits the development of final consonants, because the child has not developed space for them.

Pre-diphthongs

The ability to diphthongize begins with a child's ability to say one single vowel twice in a row. Such a pattern is common. Parents and young children use it for a variety of common expressions. Consider the following:

- *oh-oh* as a sound of concern
- *oo-oo* as a sound made by an owl
- *ee-ee* as the sound of a mouse
- *uh-uh* meaning "no-no"
- *ah-ah* meaning "Don't touch"

Real Diphthongs

Diphthongs become more sophisticated as children learn to sequence two different vowels. Early words in this group usually include:

- *hi* pronounced /haɪ/
- *bye* pronounced /baɪ/
- *go* pronounced /goʊ/
- *no* pronounced /noʊ/

Created Diphthongs

Diphthongizing is critical for expressive speech development because most children actively diphthongize final vowels that don't need to be produced that way. They do so by adding *uh* after the final sound. For example:

- *two* pronounced as /tu wʌ/
- *three* pronounced as /di yʌ/
- *go* pronounced as /go wʌ/
- *my* pronounced as /ma yʌ/

Diphthongizing in this way seems to be another of the child's strategies in developing more advanced speech production methods. He adds *uh* to the end of words to over pronounce, or super articulate, his words, making it stand out in emphasis. Diphthongizing like this creates a vocalic space for emergence of the final consonant.

Facilitating Diphthongizing

Incorporate all techniques described as Focusing on Words in action skill 3c: "Releasing."

ACTION SKILL 5F

Shortening

Shortening refers to a child's ability to shorten his vowel productions to produce the so-called "short" vowels—/ɪ/, /ɛ/, /æ/, /ʊ/, /ɔ/, and /ʌ/. Shortening adds six new vowels to his repertoire, thus completing his line of vowel development. With these short vowels, a child can produce many new words and he can produce old words better. For example:

- *big* may have been produced /biɡ/ but now can be /bɪɡ/
- *cat* may have been produced /kɑt/ but now can be /kæt/
- *book* may have been /buk/ but now can be /bʊk/

Facilitating Shortening

Incorporate all the techniques described in Focusing on Words in action skills 3c "Releasing."

Stage 6
Advancing

Leaping Beyond Simple Syllable Constructions

DURING THIS SIXTH STAGE of phoneme development, children leap forward in their expressive abilities by producing gross forms of connected speech. They also learn the pinnacle of syllable structures: CVC.

ACTION SKILLS
- jargoning
- word jargoning
- whispering
- tripling
- enclosing

ACTION SKILL 6A
Jargoning

Jargon is unintelligible prespeech behavior that sounds like connected speech in terms of length, syllable, stress, and intonation. Some call it "gibberish." Children jargon while talking to themselves, pretending to speak on the telephone, pretending to read a book aloud, singing children's songs, and talking to adults and other children. Jargon is a child's way of producing connected speech before they have enough words or phonological skills to do so. Jargon should not be ignored or discouraged. It is not unintelligible speech; it is pretend speech. Jargon begins to appear at about the same time that children begin other means of pretending.

Most children begin to jargon after they have learned to produce neat and intelligible single words and two-word combinations. Jargon is the way children try to leap past their first single words. This is evidence that the child is moving beyond these simple productions. Jargon should be viewed as advanced expressive work and not a step backward from the syllable structures of the prior stage.

Jargon is not repetitious by syllable the way babbling is. In fact, distinct syllables may or may not be heard in jargon. Also, phonological structure can be heard within jargon, but individual phonemes are randomly, and somewhat chaotically, presented. Intonation patterns used in jargon cause utterances that sound like statements, questions, requests, demands, refusals, and more.

Encouraging Jargon

Jargon can and should be encouraged. We can help it along by:

1. READING ALOUD: Read storybooks aloud to children so they can hear long stretches of connected speech. Encourage the child to "read" storybooks to you. Expect him to do so in jargon.

2. SINGING: Children often begin jargoning as they try to produce the words of songs. Include both children's and ear-catching adult songs. Let children "sing" before they know any of the words to a song. Sing and jargon along with them.

3. TALKING ON THE TELEPHONE: Play telephone together with real, toy, homemade, or pretend telephones. Take turns "talking" to one another in long continuous remarks.

4. ACTING: Some children are very expressive by nature and become exceedingly so when they

learn to jargon as an action skill. Take advantage of this natural tendency and encourage many types of pretend play during which the child can jargon to his heart's content.

5. TELL ME ALL ABOUT IT: Jargon is encouraged when we ask children to "tell me all about" a topic they love. With jargon they can tell us about toys, pictures, events, television programs, movies, birthday parties, trips to the zoo, and vacations months before they are able to do so with words. This occurs when we accept their jargon as having real communicative value.

6. MAKE A NEUTRAL RESPONSE: Often the jargon is so unintelligible and the real words are so chaotic in their presentation we can only respond with an empty word or phrase, such as, "Oh", "Really," "Is that right?" or "Hmmm." Don't worry. Let the child jargon, and respond to him with positive affirmations.

7. DEALING WITH FRUSTRATION: Some children get quite frustrated when they jargon and we don't understand them. Place the burden upon yourself. "I'm sorry. Mommy doesn't understand." Then tell the child to show you or take you to what he wants. There is no way to avoid these frustrating moments completely, so don't let them haunt you. And don't speak incessantly about them. Simply let them go and move on. Later, if you realize what the child was trying to say to you, acknowledge it to the child and develop some way for him to communicate this idea to you later on. For example, say, "Oh! You were telling me

about your lunch. You left your lunchbox at school! Next time you want to tell me about your lunchbox, go to the place where we keep it in the kitchen." Frustration is abated when picture and sign communication systems are employed at home and at school. The picture or sign system helps develop successful communication while you are waiting for the child's sound system to improve. So for example, you and the child could draw a picture about the forgotten lunchbox using simple stick drawings of the school, the lunchbox, the school bus, and so forth. The picture can be placed in a notebook or hung on the wall for all to see. Then the picture can become a medium through which the child and others can communicate about the lunchbox incident. For example, the child can be told, "Go tell grandma about your lunchbox problem." The child can tell his story to anyone willing to listen through pictures. Add more pictures as life's events unfold.

8. POOR JARGON: It should be noted that children with apraxia and dysarthria often move into jargoning before they have many consonants and vowels. As a result, their jargon often is filled with many unclear vowels and very few consonants. And their jargon sounds poor as a result. True jargon is filled with many clearly identifiable phonemes. Jargon should be encouraged even if it is void of good sounds. But clear phonemes should continue to be stimulated with other action skills.

ACTION SKILL 6B

Word Jargoning

Shortly after it appears, jargon usually begins to include embedded real words. Sometimes real words punctuate the end of jargoned phrase units. Other times, real words appear sporadically throughout jargon. Certain words and phrases tend to appear many times throughout a jargon unit. For example, one might hear phrases like *mommy did* or *I like* . . . while a child is jargoning. Early singing usually sounds like jargon embedded with real words.

Encouraging Word Jargoning

1. CONTINUE JARGON TECHNIQUES: Continue all the techniques listed above in action skill 6a: "Jargon."

2. SINGING: Singing is probably the best way to encourage word jargoning. The natural beat and rhythmic qualities of song make certain

words stand out. In "Row Your Boat", each time the word *row* comes about, sing it loud and clear. Mumble through the rest. After a while, emphasize the word *boat*, and so forth.

3. RESPOND TO THE EMBEDDED REAL WORDS: Repeat back to your child the real words you heard embedded within your child's jargon. Use these words as jump-off points in your dialogue. If the child says, "[Mumble-mumble-mumble-mumble] doggie!" you can say back, "The doggie!" or something to let the child know you heard everything he said. Often we must make a complete guess as to the child's utterance, but we can get close if we pay attention to content.

Action Skill 6c
Whispering

To *whisper* means to produce speech softly and without any voice. Whispering, as it occurs in the development of speech in young children, consists of both voiceless real words and voiceless jargon. Whispering is an advancement of the child's ability to produce the voiceless popping and raspberry sounds from Stage 3. Whispering is an important element of expressive speech development because it makes the hissing sounds stand out. Whispering encourages children to listen carefully to these sounds. In turn, this develops their ability to discriminate one from another.

Even though whispering generally comes in after the early voiceless sounds make their appearance, children who have yet to learn any voiceless sounds sometimes can be taught to do so by learning to whisper first.

Encouraging Whispering

1. MODEL IT: Whispering is encouraged by modeling.

2. MAKE IT SALIENT: Whisper to each other through tubes and funnels in order to amplify it. Also whisper in boxes, bowls, and other small spaces.

3. EAR TICKLING: Whispering to one another directly into the ear or through tubes often causes tickling of the ear as the air passes. This makes the activity giggly and fun. Take advantage of this.

4. TELL SECRETS: Tell each other secrets or pretend to do so.

5. JOKES: Whisper jokes to one another.

6. RHYMES: Whisper rhyming words or whole rhymes to one another.

7. WINDOWS AND MIRRORS: Whisper words on cold windows and mirrors to watch the steam appear on the glass.

ACTION SKILL 6D
Tripling

Tripling refers to a child's ability to produce three syllables in sequence for the production of words or phrases. Triple-syllable words and phrases are sequenced together out of all the different syllable structures they have learned to date. At least the following combinations are used:

- V V V—*Santa Claus* pronounced /æ ʌ ɔ/
- CV V V—*Grandpa Jones* pronounced /gæ ʌ o/
- V CV V—*apple juice* pronounced /æ pu u/
- V V CV—*Seattle* pronounced /i æ go/
- V V VC—*elephant* pronounced /ɛ ʌ ɪn/
- VC VC VC—*lift and load* pronounced /ɪf ɪn od/
- V CV CV—*banana* pronounced /ʌ næ nʌ/
- CV CV CV—*fishing pole* pronounced /fɪ fɪ po/

Encouraging Tripling
Incorporate all techniques described in Focusing on Words in action skill 3c: "Releasing." Also include the following:

1. MODEL: Tripling is encouraged when three-syllable words and phrases are modeled.

2. ACCEPT: Tripling is encouraged when three-syllable utterances are accepted as intelligible even when the consonants or vowels in the utterance are misrepresented.

3. MARK THE SYLLABLES WITH GESTURES: Use your head, arms, feet, or whole body to mark the three syllables of the tripled utterance. Bang on the table once for each syllable or nod your head in rhythm. Clap or stamp your foot to the three syllables. Make the syllable-ness stand out.

4. MARK THE SYLLABLES WITH BLOCKS: Place three blocks in front of the child. Have him tap one time on each block for each syllable. Hold his hand in yours to teach him how. Also use three marks on a paper, three stuffed animals in a row, three cushions on the couch, and so forth.

5. CREATE A SMALL SET: Develop a small set of three-syllable words and phrases that are practiced often. Make a picture book of the words and phrases to practice during story-book times. Consider using:

a.	elephant	g.	I want that
b.	telephone	h.	I see you
c.	ferry boat	i.	Cookie, please
d.	kitty cat	j.	Baby Mike
e.	I love you	k.	Christmas tree
f.	I don't know	l.	Hanukkah

ACTION SKILL 6E

Enclosing

The pinnacle of syllable production is the closed syllable—the CVC. A child's ability to release a syllable with a consonant, combined with his ability to close a syllable with a consonant, is finally combined together to allow the child to enclose a vowel completely with a consonant on either side. In other words, the CV and the VC together make a CVC.

But the CVC is far more advanced than either the CV or the VC. By the time the CVC emerges, children should have the capacity to produce almost all the vowels and most of the consonants. The CVC concludes all syllable development up until now, and it marks the child's entry into stage 7, the final stage of phoneme development. The CVC is used alone and in combination with all the other syllable forms incorporated to date.

CVCs can and should be produced with a wide variety of consonants and vowels. However, it is important to realize that although the vowels should be correct, the consonants can be freely substituted one for another when the CVC pattern is first acquired. Consider the following examples of early CVC productions. Note the consistent vowel pronunciations. Also, note the variations in consonants used in the pronunciation samples.

- *tape* as /teɪp/, /teɪt/, /peit/, /teik/, etc.
- *shop* as /shɑp/, /shɑk/, /tɑp/, /chɑp/, etc.
- *dog* as /dɔg/, /gɔd/, /gɔg/, /dɔd/, etc.
- *gun* as /gʌm/, /dʌn/, /gʌŋ/, /dʒʌn/, etc.
- *cat* as /kæt/, /dæt/, /tæt/, /tʃæt/, /kæk/, etc.

With the ability to produce the CVC, children begin to force many more sophisticated words into this pattern.

- *scratch* pronounced /tæθ/
- *balloon* pronounced /bun/
- *flowers* pronounced /fous/
- *helicopter* pronounced /kap/
- *hippopotamus* pronounced /mus/

The ability to produce the CVC extends to two-syllable word constructions. In this case, the utterances are made with an opening vowel followed by the CVC. This results in a V CVC construction.

- *all done* pronounced /ɔ dʌn/
- *cookies* pronounced /u dit/
- *teacher* pronounced /i tut/
- *ABCs* pronounced /eɪ dit/
- *St. Louis* pronounced /eɪ dus/

The ability to produce the CVC also extends to the ability to say words with two-syllable CV CVC constructions.

- *busses* pronounced as /bʌ dɪt/
- *helicopter* pronounced as /kɑ tɚ/
- *ambulance* pronounced as /bæ mus/
- *fire truck* pronounced as /bɑ dʌk/
- *bad guys* pronounced as /bæ daɪs/
- *ice cream* pronounced as /daɪ dim/

The ability to produce the CVC also combines with tripling to form words and phrases of three syllables with the final syllable closed. This is the CV CV CVC construction.

- *Christmas* pronounced as /ki ki mas/
- *ambulance* pronounced as /bæ bu bus/
- *fire truck* pronounced as /bɑh yʌ dʌk/
- *remote control* pronounced as /mo mo dout/
- *Don't do that* pronounced as /do du dat/

Developing the CVC

The CVC should not be targeted too early in therapy, nor should it be overworked or trained exclusively. This is because too much CVC training too early can inhibit the other action skills that should be developing.

Incorporate all techniques described in Focusing on Words in action skill 3c: "Releasing." Also include the following:

1. EXPECT CORRECT VOWELS: Encourage production of correct vowels in the CVC. If vowels are produced incorrectly, then retreat to earlier vowel work.

2. FOCUS ON THE CONSONANTS: Insist on the presence of an initial and final consonant. If the child is failing consistently in this regard, you have advanced to this skill too early or you are focusing on it too much and disregarding other earlier developing skills.

3. FREE SUBSTITUTIONS OF THE C: When first learning the CVC, allow free substitution of the initial and final consonants. You goal is to get a consonant in both places, not to get the correct ones in these places.

4. CORRECT C: Correct the consonants over time. If the child consistently produces CVCs with many consonant substitutions, stimulating the CVC should continue. However, treatment also should retreat back along the path of phoneme development to the points where he has failed to gain specific phonemes. For example, if he readily confuses /p/, /t/, and /k/ in his CVC constructions, retreat to the point in development where the child learned to differentiate stop consonants by place. That would be Stage 4: "Honing."

5. TRADITIONAL ARTICULATION AND PHONOLOGICAL THERAPY: Historic articulation and phonological therapy procedures come into play here. Focus on presenting clear models, developing auditory awareness and discrimination, and so forth. Incorporate all techniques

described in Focusing on Words in action skill 3c: "Releasing."

6. SPELLING: Include spelling work here to help children see the individual sounds that comprise the words they are rehearsing. Use three-letter words like *cat, dog, sit, mom, men, tub, run,* and so forth.

Stage 7
Finishing

Learning to Add Clusters and Frication in All Levels of Speech

BY THE END OF THIS FINAL STAGE, children are able to incorporate /l/, /r/, and /s/ clusters into all aspects of expressive speech. These are the most advanced of all the phonological skills.

ACTION SKILLS
- /w/-clustering
- syllabifying
- glide clustering
- post-vocalic /s/-clustering
- pre-vocalic /s/-clustering
- stridency overgeneralizing
- 3-consonant clustering
- advanced clustering

Therapy Techniques for Stage 7

The final stage puts the finishing touches on articulation, phonological, and oral-motor development. All the action skills a child has learned have carried him to this point. He can produce every vowel, nasal, glide, stop, and hissing sound. Now he is ready to sequence two and three consonants together to form new phonological units. As in all the development so far, these skills emerge in a systematic way. All methods of training articulation and phonological skills can be employed throughout this stage:

- model
- explain
- demonstrate
- slow down
- amplify
- bombard
- rehearse
- drill
- use a mirror for visual feedback
- play with words
- rhyme words
- use visual and tactile cues for phonemes
- incorporate spelling practice
- produce target words in phrases, sentences, and conversation.

Action Skill 7a
/w/-**Clustering**

Most children begin to cluster with /w/, using it as a substitution for /l/ and /r/ in blends of their kind. For example, children say /bwu/ for *blue*, and /gwin/ for *green*. The w/l and w/r substitutions are natural because /w/ is the easiest glide and /l/ and /r/ are the most difficult ones.

/w/-clustering should not be considered a problem when it emerges. It is a specific developmental skill that functions as a bridge between consonant singletons and true clusters. /w/-clustering should be encouraged in order to lead the child toward more advanced cluster productions.

R-Clusters
Two-consonant clusters constructed with /r/ include /pr/, /br/, /tr/, /dr/, /kr/, and /gr/. These should be practiced with /w/ as a substitute for /r/.

- /pr/—*pretty* pronounced /pwɪti/
- /br/—*brown* pronounced /bwoʊn/
- /tr/—*train* pronounced /tweɪn/
- /dr/—*drum* pronounced /dwʌm/
- /kr/—*crazy* pronounced /kweɪzi/
- /gr/—*green* pronounced /gwin/

L-Clusters

Two-consonant clusters constructed with /l/ include /pl/, /bl/, /kl/, and /gl/. These should be practiced with /w/ as a substitute for /l/.

- /pl/—*please* pronounced /pwiz/
- /bl/—*black* pronounced /bwæk/
- /kl/—*clock* pronounced /kwɑk/
- /gl/—*glass* pronounced /gwæs/

W-Clusters

Clustering with /w/ also includes mature clusters of /tw/, /dw/, /kw/, and /gw/.

- /tw/—Tweedy Bird, twelve, twenty, twinkle, Twinkie
- /dw/—dweeb, dwarf, dwell, dwelling, dwindle, Duane
- /kw/—quarter, question, quiet, quit, quaint, quart, quint
- /gw/—Gwen, Gwenneth

Action Skill 7b

Syllabifying

Syllabifying is the addition of a schwa to create a full syllable out of a consonant cluster that employs /l/ or /r/. For example, *blue* is pronounced /bʌ lu/, and *brown* is pronounced /bʌ raun/. Syllabifying also is used with /w/-clustering when that skill is just emerging. For example, in early speech development *blue* often is pronounced /bʌ wu/.

Syllabifying is a specific skill learned on the path toward complete cluster production. It should be encouraged when the time has arrived to add clusters to the repertoire. Inserting a vowel in the midst of a cluster makes the cluster easier to produce because it gives the child more time to transition from the first to the second consonant within the cluster. The transition from the first to the second consonant is easier. Syllabifying should be taught when children are having difficulty assimilating /l/ and /r/ clusters. Teach syllabifying with /w/, /l/, and /r/—in that order.

Action Skill 7c
Glide Clustering

Glide clustering is the use of /l/ and /r/ in syllable-initial blends produced without /w/-clustering or syllabifying. The oral movements required for mature /l/ and /r/ blends are highly skilled ones. They develop toward the end of the pathway of phoneme development. The co-articulatory effects are substantial, and there is almost a simultaneous oral positioning for the first and second consonants in each cluster. Most children take an extended period of time transitioning from /w/-clustering and syllabifying to mature /l/ and /r/ clustering. Consonant clusters constructed with /r/ include /pr/, /br/, /tr/, /dr/, /kr/, and /gr/. Consonant clusters constructed with /l/ include /pl/, /bl/, /kl/, and /gl/.

ACTION SKILL 7D

Postvocalic /s/-Clustering

A postvocalic /s/-cluster contains an /s/ produced after another consonant at the end of a word. Postvocalic /s/-clusters develop early, usually far earlier than their prevocalic counterparts. This is because it is easier to off-glide into a hissing sound than it is to on-glide with one. Postvocalic /s/-clusters include: /ps/, /bs/, /ts/, /ds/, /ks/, /gs/, /ms/, /ns/, /ŋs/, /ws/, /ls/, /ys/, /rs/. Please note the following:

- An /s/ following a voiced consonant usually is produced with voicing, thus changing a word like *cans* to be pronounced /kænz/.
- The postvocalic /s/-cluster that is the earliest to emerge usually is /ts/. This is because it requires the least oral movement in the transition.
- Words that end in one of the anterior hissing sounds—/f/, /v/, /θ/, /ð/—are extremely

difficult to pronounce and will emerge quite late. Consider the words *cuffs*, *gloves*, *baths*, *bathes*.

- Words that end with a lingual hissing phoneme—/s/, /z/, /ʃ/, /ʒ/, /tʃ/, and /dʒ/—will be pronounced by making the final /s/ into an additional syllable. Consider *busses*, *buzzes*, *bushes*, *beiges*, *matches*, and *edges*. Each of these constructions changes the postvocalic /s/-cluster into a CVC syllable, thus eradicating the need to cluster so difficult a sequence.

Morphemes

A post-vocalic /s/-cluster is a highly valuable tool in language development. Postvocalic /s/-clusters are used for the important morphemes that emerge between eighteen months and three years of age.

- PLURAL: lights, cakes, fans
- POSSESSIVE: mom's car, dad's shoe, cat's meow
- CONTRACTED COPULAR: That's good. It's all right. What's that?
- CONTRACTED AUXILIARY: The man's coming. What's going on? It's turning around.
- THIRD PERSON REGULAR TENSE VERBS: He bats now. She wants it. That looks funny.

Action Skill 7e

Prevocalic /s/-**Clustering**

Prevocalic /s/-clusters are consonant clusters in which /s/ is the first sound. These include /sp/, /st/, /sk/, /sm/, /sn/, /sl/, and /sw/. Most children delete the initial /s/ when they are learning words that require an initial /s/-cluster, such as in *spoon, star, skate, smoke, snake, slide*, and *sweater*. Most children develop prevocalic /s/-clusters months after their postvocalic counterparts emerge.

Mid Word /s/-Clusters

Prevocalic /s/-clusters also occur in the middle of words, as in *Casper, mister, masking*, and *mismatch*. The advanced nature of these word concepts and their oral-motor requirements render them to later development.

Across Words

Prevocalic /s/-clusters also occur across words in phrases or sentences. Consider the /s/-clusters that occur in the following:

- "I mi<u>ss T</u>om."
- "He's on bu<u>s n</u>ine."
- "That's my pa<u>ss t</u>icket."

ACTION SKILL 7F

Stridency Overgeneralizing

The emergence of prevocalic and postvocalic /s/-clustering usually coincides with a period of stridency overgeneralization. This means that the hissing sounds are overused, reduplicated, assimilated, and added as extra sounds within words. For example:

- *Santa Clause* pronounced /ʃæ nʌ ʃɔʃ/
- *bus* pronounced /sʌs/
- *spinach* pronounced /fɪ fʌf/
- *spoon* pronounced /θpuθ/
- *alligators* pronounced /ʃæ ʌ ʃeɪ ɚʃ/

Overusing /s/ and other hissing sounds should be viewed as a normal process of speech sound acquisition. In fact, the overuse of hissing sounds should be encouraged when children enter this phase. Overusing the hissing phonemes allows children to embed these sounds into words and connected speech when they otherwise couldn't. Overuse of the hissing sounds will dominate for a short while, after which the child will begin to eliminate the excess.

While children are in the phase of stridency overgeneralization, they tend to freely substitute one hissing sound for another. Instead of viewing this as a problem, we see this as the child's ability to incorporate frication into his spontaneous utterances. But the child has not learned to differentiate these sounds by place of articulation. He has not landed on the right place of production for each individual phoneme. This usually results in wild and seemingly random substitutions of one hissing phoneme for another. During the course of a week or month, a child may overgeneralize by pronouncing *soap* with an initial /f/, /θ/, /s/, /ʃ/, or /tʃ/. On the word *zoo*, he might use an initial /v/, /ð/, /z/, /ʒ/, or /dʒ/. Traditional articulation literature labeled these errors as inconsistent and random. Today, we know these sounds occur predictably according to the action skill being learned—the action of overgeneralizing. Overgeneralizing should be encouraged when it emerges.

3-Consonant Clustering

Three-consonant clusters are constructed with a combination of /s/, /l/, /r/, and /w/ clusters. They include:

- /spl/—splash
- /spr/—spring
- /str/—street
- /skr/—scratch
- /skw/—squeak

Syllable Final Sequences

Three-consonant clusters also include syllable-final sequences, like

- /ndl/ and /ndlz/—handle, handles
- /mbl/ and /mblz/—mumble, mumbles
- /ngl/ and /nglz/—single, singles

Clearly, it takes full control of all the skills learned until now to combine consonant phonemes in this way. It takes months, even years, for children to straighten out the possible combinations of phonemes necessary to produce these advanced clusters.

Order of Emergence

Phonemes /l/ and /r/ usually are the last to emerge in three-consonant clusters. For example, it is common for children to change the word *splash*, with its /spl/ cluster, to /spwæʃ/. But it is quite unusual for them to change it to /plæʃ/. The /s/ often comes in earlier than the /l/ or /r/.

ACTION SKILL 7H
Advanced Clustering

The final element of phoneme development involves a child's ability to sequence every conceivable set of consonants within words and across words. The total number of consonants that can be sequenced usually is five. A complicated sequence like /ndlsk/ can occur in a sentence like "He can ha<u>ndle</u> <u>sch</u>ool." It would be impossible for a child to produce such a complicated sequence if he could not produce each phoneme of the sequence individually and if he could not produce the simple two- and three-consonant clusters discussed above.

It is difficult to understand the conversation of children who have problems sequencing at this high level even though they may produce individual phonemes and words well. Rapid conversational speech will be marked by the deletion of individual consonants and whole syllables. With unknown topics the result will be low intelligibility, especially if the client

speaks fast. Treatment should be geared toward help-
ing the child learn to sequence smoothly from one
consonant to another. Syllabifying clusters, making
sure the child is diphthongizing and making syllables
in rhythmic ways are is important elements of this
treatment.

Facilitating the Final Skill

Remediation at this level focuses on subtle skills.

1. SHORE UP EARLIER SKILLS: Make sure the child
   has full control over the two- and three-consonant clusters described above.
2. SLOW DOWN: This child is speaking too fast
   for his oral-motor abilities. He needs to slow
   his speech to a rate that matches his abilities.
   Work on exaggerating the beat properties of
   speech. Help him punch out syllables. Then
   encourage him to increase speed while main-
   taining accuracy.
3. EAR TRAINING: This final level of articulation
   therapy requires a deep level of ear training. The child must learn to monitor his own
   speech during rapid conversation. Work on
   words, phrases, sentences, and conversation.
   And make him judge his own utterances.
   "How did you do on that one?" All these children have a great deal of difficulty with this
   task. They need to be carefully led to a place
   where they can do their own auditory self-
   monitoring.

Seven Stages Outline

Stage 1. Preparing: Getting the Voice Ready for Speech

A. Action Skill 1A. Voicing

1. Act of producing voice
2. Produces the QRN
   a. High
   b. Mid
   c. Unrounded
   d. Nasalized
   e. Vowel
   f. Short Duration

THERAPY TOOLS

1. Speech Activation Toys
2. Kazoos
3. Flexible Tubes
4. Funnels
5. Small Echo Chambers
6. Large Echo Chambers
7. Synchronous Vocalizations
8. Mutual Imitation

      9. Singing
      10. Rough House and Gross Motor Play
      11. Horns, Whistles and Sirens
      12. Sensitivity
      13. Oral Strength
      14. Dialogue

B. Action Skill 1B. Prolonging

1. Act of extending length of vocal production; sustaining voice
2. Producing a long QRN
3. Requires deeper inhalation and extended exhalation
4. Foundation for all development from here on

THERAPY TOOLS

1. Continue all voice and airflow stimulation activities as described above.
2. Prolongation Whistles

C. Action Skill 1c: Differentiating

1. Activating the velopharyngeal mechanism
2. Result: differentiated oral sound and nasal sound
3. Requires prolonged sound

THERAPY TOOLS

1. Continue all voice and airflow stimulation activities as described above.
2. Modifications to flexible tubes
3. Terminology: "Make the sound come out your nose (or mouth)."
4. Accept any oral or nasal sound
5. Model and encourage the child to say /ŋ/.

D. Action Skill 1d. Posturing

1. Act of positioning the mouth in basic ways while prolonging sound

2. Alters the oral and nasal sounds
   a. Open — /ɑ/
   b. Close — /m/
   c. Smile — /i/
   d. Pucker — /u/
   e. Round —/o/
   f. Closed at tongue — /n/

THERAPY TOOLS
1. Continue all voice and airflow stimulation activities as described above.
2. Jaw Mobility
3. Jaw Stability
4. Oral-Motor Techniques
5. Feeding Techniques
6. Vocabulary

Stage 2. Speechifying: Making Utterances Sound Speech-like

A. Action Skill 2a. Projecting
1. Act of making voice a little louder and projecting it further out body; internal bearing down process
2. Oral shout; less infantile nasals

THERAPY TOOLS
1. Continue all voice and airflow stimulation activities as described above.
2. Modeling
3. Amplifiers
4. Large Spaces
5. Concepts
6. Restrict the Loud Voice

B. Action Skill 2b. Pitching
1. Act of altering rate of vocal fold vibration: lengthen/shorten vocal folds

2. Changes pitch
   a. High: squeal
   b. Low: growl
   c. Mid: all else in between

THERAPY TOOLS
   1. Continue all voice and airflow stimulation activities as described above.
   2. Modeling
   3. Toys
   4. Natural Gestures
   5. Animal sounds

C. Action Skill 2c. Intoning
   1. Act of altering pitch in speech-like fashion
   2. Done within a single vocalization

THERAPY TOOLS
   1. Continue all voice and airflow stimulation activities as described above.
   2. Modeling
   3. Gesture Cues
   4. Establish Specific Patterns

D. Action Skill 2d. Pulsing
   1. Act of creating the first syllable-like markings
   2. Pulsing develops as children learn to move in rhythmic way
      a. trunk, head, arms, legs
      b. develops gross to fine

THERAPY TOOLS
   1. Continue all voice and airflow stimulation activities as described above.
   2. Bouncing
   3. Hands and Knees
   4. Trunk Flexing
   5. Kicking the Legs

6. Arm Flapping
7. Modeling

E. Action Skill 2e. Laughing
1. Act of laughing
2. Exercising deep inhalation and extensive sound prolongation
3. The longest of the prolonged sounds
4. Loud: oral or nasal; wide swings in pitch/ intonation

THERAPY TOOLS
1. Continue all voice and airflow stimulation activities as described above.
2. Laugh Yourself
3. Find the Trigger
4. Frequency
5. Avoid Assumptions about Tickling

Stage 3. Honing: Zeroing in on Non-Vocalic Consonants Differentiated by Place

A. Action Skill 3a. Vibrating
1. Act of constricting loosely along the vocal tract: Raspberry (RSP)
2. RSPs are both voiced and voiceless
3. RSPs establish place of articulation from anterior to posterior
4. RSPs establish eggressive air and voice movement
5. The full list of RSPs:
   a. RSP-1: a voiceless raspberry made at the lips (bilabial)
   b. RSP-2: a voiced raspberry made at the lips (bilabial)
   c. RSP-3: a voiceless raspberry made with tongue-tip and lips (lingua-labial)

    d.   RSP-4: a voiced raspberry made with tongue-tip and lips (lingua-labial)

    e.   RSP-5: a voiceless raspberry made at t-back and velum (lingua-velar)

    f.   RSP-6: a voiced raspberry made at tongue-back and velum (lingua-velar)

    g.   RSP-7: a voiceless raspberry made in the trachea (tracheal)

    h.   RSP-8: a voiced raspberry made in the trachea (tracheal)

    i.   RSP-9: a voiceless raspberry made at the glottis (glottal)

    j.   RSP-10: a voiced raspberry made at the glottis (glottal)

    k.   RSP-11: a raspberry made in the nose (the "snort"; usually ingressive)

THERAPY TOOLS

1. Continue all voice and airflow stimulation activities as described above.
2. Raspberry Blower: to teach concept
3. Jaw Stability: jaw must be high
4. Experiment with place: practice them all
5. Models: Make sure to model all these sounds yourself.
6. Visual, Tactile and Auditory Cues
7. Feeding Therapy: purees
8. Spitting: experience but discourage
9. Assign Meaning
   a. Bilabial raspberries can be used for motor sounds.
   b. Lingua-labial raspberries can be used to indicate rejection.
   c. Lingua-velar raspberries can be used for crashing sounds.
   d. Tracheal raspberries can be used for animal growls.
   e. Glottal raspberries can be used to represent the scary noises of monsters.
10. Label Place of Articulation: at client level

B. Action Skill 3b. Occluding

1. Act of adding more tension to the raspberries
2. Completely occluding the air stream at each place: stopping airflow
3. No consonants produced: none released

THERAPY TOOLS

1. Continue all voice and airflow stimulation activities as described above.
2. Continue Raspberry Techniques
3. Increase Oral Tension; squeeze
4. Jaw Stability; jaw high
5. Mechanical Occlusion; objects used to stop airflow

C. Action Skill 3c. Releasing

1. Act of releasing occluded positions
   by quickly lowering the jaw after pressure builds
2. Gross production of CVs — with voiced consonants and neutral vowels
   a. /b/+Vowel
   b. /d/+Vowel
   c. /g/+Vowel
   d. /ʔ/+Vowel
   e. /m/+vowel
   f. /n/+vowel
   g. /ŋ/+vowel
3. Neutral vowels become the vowels he learned earlier — /i/, /u/, /ɑ/ and /o/; e.g., /bɑ/, /bi/, /bu/, /bo/, /dɑ/, /di/, /du/, /do/, etc.
4. CV Words: e.g.,
   a. boo, bee, b, bow
   b. do, dough, dee, day, duh
   c. goo, go
   d. me, may, moo, mow, ma (mom)
   e. nee, nay, new, no
5. Other Simple Words:
   a. e.g., "bye" pronounced /bɑ/

  b.   e.g., "car" pronounced /kɑ/
  c.   e.g., "boat" pronounced /bo/
6. Complex Words: e.g., "sugar cookies" pronounced /gu/
7. Phrases: "There he is" pronounced /de•/ with inflection

THERAPY TOOLS
  1. Continue all voice and airflow stimulation activities as described above.
  2. Continue working on occlusion
  3. Jaw Lowering
  4. Objects to teach the concept of building up inter oral air pressure
  5. Glottal Release

D. Action Skill 3d. Popping

1. Act of releasing occluded positions with air only (no voice)
2. Create phonemes /p/, /t/ and /k/
3. Ingressive and eggressive at first

THERAPY TOOLS
  1. Continue all voice and airflow stimulation activities as described above.
  2. Continue working on raspberries and occlusion
  3. Jaw Lowering
  4. Objects to build inter oral air pressure
  5. Glottal Release

E. Action Skill 3e. Fricating

1. Act of refining raspberry vibrations (toward fine motor control)
2. Clumsy productions of /f/, /v/, /θ/, /ð/, /s/, /z/, /ʃ/, /ʒ/, /tʃ/, /dʒ/ and /h/

3. Phonemes are very unstable by place: place is not "locked in"
4. Ingressive and eggressive at first
5. Single sounds produced

THERAPY TOOLS

1. Continue all voice and airflow stimulation activities as described above.
2. Model
3. Amplification
4. Assign Meaning
   a. /f/ — the sound of a cat's wrath
   b. /v/ — the sound of a speed boat motor
   c. /s/ — the sound of a snake's hiss
   d. /z/ — the sound of a buzzing bee
   e. /ʃ/ — the sound meaning "Be quiet."
   f. /ʒ/ — the sound of an airplane motor
   g. /tʃ/ — the "chew-chew" sound of an old train
   h. /dʒ/ — the sound of jumping
   i. /h/ — the sound of being worn out

F. Action Skill 3f. Vowelizing

1. Act of producing long vowel sounds purposefully altered, e.g., "Ahhhhhheeeeohhhuhhhhwwwooooo"
2. Tunes the ear to subtle variations in vowel sound

THERAPY TOOLS

1. Breath control
2. Speech response toys
3. Tubes
4. Songs
5. Counting
6. Alphabet

Stage 4. Oscillating: Creating Sequences with Reciprocating Oral Movements

A. Action Skill 4a. Jaw Babbling

1. Act of oscillating gross jaw movements while pro-longing voice: jaw moves in a big up-and-down pattern (gross movement)
2. A huge number of specific new vocal patterns emerge
3. Names of new sounds correspond to their actions
   a. mahing
   b. emming
   c. nahing
   d. enning
   e. ngahing
   f. enging
   g. numming
   h. ngumming
   i. ah-ing
   j. oo-ing
   k. ee-ing
   l. oh-ing
   m. ai-ing
   n. uh-ing
   o. lalling
   p. lateral lalling

THERAPY TOOLS

1. Continue all voice and airflow stimulation activi-ties as described above.
2. Jaw Movement: Get the jaw to move up and down
3. Oral Postures: Continue to establish the specific oral postures

B. Action Skill 4b. Silent Sequencing

1. Act of oscillating jaw movements while moving air (no voice)
2. Ingressive and eggressive air movement is noted: panting
3. Outward moving air begins to dominate as oscillation skills advance
4. "Pre-whispering"
5. Some made with big up-and-down jaw movements — /p/, /t/, /k/, /tʃ/
6. Some made with jaw held high — /f/, /θ/, /s/, /ʃ/
7. One made with jaw held low — /h/
8. One made with jaw elevated (mouth closed) — sniffing

THERAPY TOOLS

1. Continue all voice and airflow stimulation activities as described above.
2. Jaw Movement: Get the jaw to move up and down
3. Panting: inhale and exhale in short, rapid sequences
4. Oral Postures: Continue to establish the specific oral postures

C. Action Skill 4c. Lip Babbling

1. Act of oscillating lip movements while prolonging voice
2. Made while the jaw is held high and lightly clenched
3. "Oo-ee-ing" results when the lips pucker and retract in sequence
4. "Woo-ing" results when the lips pucker and release in sequence

THERAPY TOOLS
1. Continue all voice and airflow stimulation activities as described above.
2. Activate the Lips: Get them to pucker, round and retract
3. Elevate the Jaw: Get it high and strong. Teach the client to clench.

D. Action Skill 4d. Tongue Babbling

1. Act of oscillating tongue movements while prolonging sound
2. Made while the mouth is open
3. Differentiates tongue movements from jaw movements
4. Voiceless trials sneak in on occasion but true Tongue Babbling is voiced
   a. blubbling
   b. blalling
   c. dlelling
   d. lerring
   e. blerring
   f. lateral lerring

THERAPY TOOLS
1. Continue all voice and airflow stimulation activities as described above.
2. Jaw Stability: Open his mouth wide and to hold the jaw low.
3. Tongue Mobility: Get the tongue to move out , in, forward, back, left, right
4. Vocabulary: Establish one label to describe each action
5. Move the tongue without voice

E. Action Skill 4e. Classic Babbling

1. Act of sequencing consonants (C) and vowels (V)
2. Well-defined repeating syllables: "CV CV CV…"

3. Made while prolonging voice; therefore, voiced
   C's only
   a. Nasals (/m/, /n/, /ŋ/)
   b. Glides (/w/, /l/, /y/, /r/)
   c. Voiced stops (/b/, /d/, /g/)
   d. Five basic vowels /ɑ/, /i/, /u/, /o/, /ʌ/
4. Devoid of the intonation and stress patterns
5. An amusing way to capture an audience

THERAPY TOOLS
1. Continue all voice and airflow stimulation activities as described above.
2. Model: Model sequences for the child to hear and see.
3. Baby Play: Pretending to be babies; dolls
4. Challenges: "I bet you can't say…"
5. Forbidding Babbling: "Don't say…" with a gleam in your eye.
6. Alphabet Sounds
7. Puppets: A frog puppet can say "Guh-guh-guh", etc.

F. Action Skill 4f. Advanced Babbling

1. Act of babbling with voiceless stops
   a. /p/, /t/, /k/
2. Act of babbling with hissing sounds
   a. /f/, /v/, /θ/, /ð/, /s/, /z/, /ʃ/, /ʒ/, /tʃ/, /dʒ/, /h/
3. Rare in normal development; often necessary in therapy
4. Void of intonation and stress patterns

THERAPY TOOLS
1. Continue all procedures for Classic Babbling above with the new sounds

Stage 5. Solidifying: Establishing Basic Syllable Constructions

A. Action Skill 5a. Embedding

1. Act of placing a consonant sound between two vowel sounds
2. Act of moving in to and away from a constriction: VCV pattern
3. Words, protowords and protophrases
   a. Words: e.g., "open" produced /o pɛ/
   b. Protowords: e.g., "elephant" produced /ɛ nɛ/
   c. Protophrases: e.g., "What's that?" produced /ʌ dæ/?
4. Free substitution of one consonant for another

B. Action Skill 5b. Closing

1. Act of closing a syllable; moving from open to constriction
2. Results in the VC construction
   a. Voiceless stops (/p/, /t/, /k/)
   b. Voiceless hissing sounds (/f/, /θ/, /s/, /ʃ/, /tʃ/)
   c. Voiced nasals (/m/, /n/, /ŋ/)
3. Simple VC words: "up", "eat", "out", "ick!", "on" and "off"
4. Modified simple words: "fish" produced as /ɪʃ/
5. Complex words: "elephant" produced as /ɛ•n/

C. Action Skill 5c. Duplicating

1. Act of making two identical syllables in sequence: CV CV
2. The most common way to form early words: "mama", "dada"
3. A shortening of the basic classic babbling process
4. Universal Words: "mama", "dada", "nana" and "papa"

5. Complex Words: "peanut butter" pronounced /bʌ bʌ/
6. Phrases: "fix it" produced /dɪ dɪ/

D. Action Skill 5d. Diminutizing
1. Act of creating diminutive words: CVC/i/
2. Diminutive: two-syllable words which end in "y" or "ie", e.g., "kitty", "doggie", "horsie", "birdie"
3. Easy for children to produce
4. Represents first time child produces two syllables with two different vowels
5. Common Diminutives: "mommy", "daddy", "baby" and "puppy"
6. Uncommon Diminutives: "shoesies"

E. Action Skill 5e. Diphthongizing
1. Act of producing two vowels and the gliding sounds made between them
2. Diphthongs in English: /aɪ/, /aʊ/, /ɔɪ/, /iu/, /eɪ/ e.g., "hi", "ouch", "boy", "you", "hay!"
3. Makes a child's speech sound melodious, more speech-like; allows time for intonation and stress patterns
4. Three types:
   a. Pre-diphthongs (same vowel): "o-o", "oo-oo", "ee-ee", "ah-ah", "uh-uh"
   b. Real Diphthongs: "hi", "bye", "go", "no"
   c. Created Diphthongs: adding "uh" after final V: e.g., "two" as /tu wʌ/
5. Creates a vocalic space for emergence of the final consonant

F. Action Skill 5f. Shortening
1. Act of producing the short vowels: /ɪ/, /ɛ/, /æ/, /ʊ/, /ɔ/ and /ʌ/ "pig", "get", "hat", "book", dog", "what"

2. Allows a child to produce many words with greater intelligibility: e.g., "big" may have been produced /big/ but now can be /bɪg/

Stage 6. Advancing: Leaping Beyond Simple Syllable Constructions

A. Action Skill 6a. Jargoning

1. Act of producing unintelligible prespeech behavior: "gibberish"
2. Sounds like connected speech in terms of length, syllable, stress and intonation
3. Not unintelligible speech: *pretend speech*
4. A way to leap past single words and early phrases
5. Loose phonological structure can be heard within jargon
6. Intonation patterns: statements, questions, requests, demands, refusals, etc.

THERAPY TOOLS
1. Read aloud
2. Sing
3. Telephone
4. Act
5. Tell me all about it
6. Make a neutral response
7. Deal with frustration

B. Action Skill 6b. Word-jargoning

1. Act of jargoning with embedded real words
2. Early singing often is produced this way

THERAPY TOOLS
1. Read aloud
2. Sing
3. Telephone

4. Act
5. Tell me all about it
6. Make a neutral response
7. Deal with frustration
8. Respond to the real words

C. Action Skill 6c. Whispering

1. Act of producing speech softly and without voice
2. An advancement of the voiceless popping and raspberry sounds
3. Makes the hissing sounds stand out; makes them salient
4. Develops discrimination

THERAPY TOOLS
1. Model
2. Make salient
3. Ear tickling
4. Tell secrets
5. Whisper jokes
6. Whisper rhymes
7. Windows and mirrors

D. Action Skill 6d. Tripling

1. Act of producing three syllables in sequence for words and phrases
2. Consists of every syllable structure learned to date
   a. V V V: "Santa Claus" pronounced /æ ʌ ɔ/
   b. CV V V: "Grandpa Jones" pronounced /gæ ʌ o/
   c. V CV V: "apple juice" pronounced /æ pʌ u/
   d. V V CV: "Seattle" pronounced /i æ go/
   e. V V VC: "elephant" pronounced /ɛ ʌ ɪn/
   f. VC VC VC: "Lift and load" as /ɪf ɪn oud/
   g. V CV CV: "banana" pronounced /ʌ næ nʌ/
   h. CV CV CV: "fishing pole" as /fɪ fi po/

THERAPY TOOLS
1. Model
2. Accept
3. Mark the syllables with gestures
4. Mark the syllables with objects
5. Create a small set, e.g., "I love you", "I don't know", "I see you"

E. Action Skill 6e. Enclosing

1. Act of surrounding a vowel with consonants

2. The pinnacle of syllable production; the closed syllable; the CVC: CV + VC = CVC

3. Words produced with a wide variety of consonants and vowels

    a. Vowels should be correct

    b. Consonants freely substituted one for another
    — "dog" as /dɔd/, /gɔg/, /nɔd/, /dʒɔg/, /dɔg/

4. Complex words: "flowers" pronounced /fous/

5. Also: V CVC constructions: "cookies" pronounced /u dɪt/

6. Also: CV CVC constructions: "busses" pronounced as /bʌ dɪt/

7. Also: CV CV CVC construction: "Christmas" pronounced as /ki ki mɑs/

8. Phrases: "That not mine" produced /dæ na mɑɪn/

THERAPY TOOLS
1. Expect correct V's
2. Focus on the C's
3. Free substituting of the C's
4. Correct C
5. Traditional articulation and phonological therapy
6. Spelling

Stage 7. Finishing: Learning to Add Clusters and Frication in All Levels of Speech

A. Action Skill 7a. /w/-Clustering

1. Act of producing /w/ after a consonant
2. Most common: used as a substitution for /l/ and /r/ in blends
   a. R-Clusters: /pr/, /br/, /tr/, /dr/, /kr/ and /gr/
   b. L-Clusters: /pl/, /bl/, /kl/ and /gl/
3. Functions as a bridge between consonant singletons and true clusters.
4. True /w/-Clusters: /tw/, /dw/, /kw/ and /gw/
   a. e.g., "twin", "Duane", "queen", "Gwen"

B. Action Skill 7b. Syllabifying

1. Act of adding a schwa to create a full syllable out of a consonant cluster
   a. e.g., "blue" produced /bʌ lu/
   b. e.g., "brown" produced /bʌ roun/
   c. e.g., "queen" produced /kʌ win/
   d. e.g., "train" produced /tʌ wein/
2. Makes clusters easier to produce
3. Gives more time to transition from the first to the second consonant

C. Action Skill 7c. Glide Clustering

1. Act of producing /l/ and /r/ in syllable-initial blends
   a. R-Clusters: /pr/, /br/, /tr/, /dr/, /kr/ and /gr/
   b. L-Clusters: /pl/, /bl/, /kl/ and /gl/
2. Co-articulatory effects are substantial; almost a simultaneous oral positioning for both consonants

D. Action Skill 7d. Postvocalic /s/-clustering

1. Act of producing /s/ after another consonant (end of words/syllables)
2. Includes: /ps/, /bs/, /ts/, /ds/, /ks/, /gs/, /ms/, /ns/, /ŋs/, /ws/, /ls/, /ys/, /rs/, etc.
3. Morphemes: plural, possessive, contracted copular is, contracted auxiliary is, third person regular tense verbs

E. Action Skill 7e. Prevocalic /s/-Clustering

1. Act of producing consonant clusters in which /s/ is the first sound
2. Includes: /sp/, /st/, /sk/, /sm/, /sn/, /sl/ and /sw/
3. Most children develop prevocalic /s/-clusters after postvocalic counterparts
4. Also: mid-word /s/-clusters: e.g., Casper, mister, masking
5. Also: across words: e.g., I miss Tom, He's on bus nine, That's my pass ticket

F. Action Skill 7f. Stridency Overgeneralizing

1. Act of overusing hissing sounds
   a. Substituted, reduplicated, assimilated and added as extra sounds
   b. e.g., "Santa Clause" pronounced /ʃæ nʌ ʃɔʃ/
2. A normal process
3. Allows embedding of these sounds into connected speech before ready
4. Dominates for a short while
5. Tendency is to freely substitute one hissing sound for another

G. Action Skill 7g. 3-Consonant Clustering

1. Act of constructing three-consonant clusters
   a. combines /s/, /l/, /r/ and /w/
2. Includes: /spl/, /spr/, /str/, /skr/, /skw/

3. Also: syllable-final sequences
   a. with /l/: e.g., handle, mumble, single
   b. with /r/: e.g., under

H. Action Skill 7h. Advanced Clustering

1. Act of sequencing every conceivable set of consonants within and across words
   a. Words: "po<u>nders</u>", "co<u>nju</u>res", "a<u>cts</u>", "fi<u>fths</u>", "wa<u>sps</u>", "fi<u>sts</u>"
   b. Across words: "He ca<u>n't h</u>a<u>ndle sch</u>ool."
2. Problems in this final area:
   a. Rapid rate will be marked by consonant and syllable deletion
   b. Causes children to be difficult to understand in conversation

APPENDIX B

7 Stages of Phoneme Development
by Pam Marshalla

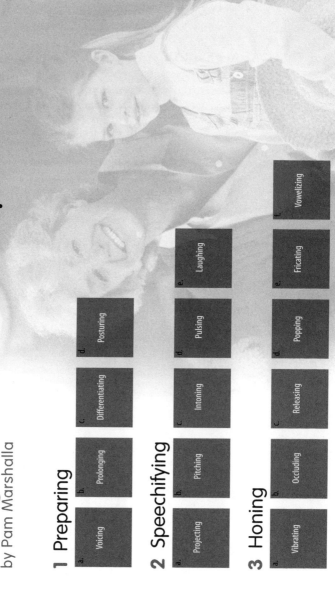

1 Preparing

a. Voicing
b. Prolonging
c. Differentiating
d. Posturing

2 Speechifying

a. Projecting
b. Pitching
c. Intoning
d. Pulsing
e. Laughing

3 Honing

a. Vibrating
b. Occluding
c. Releasing
d. Popping
e. Fricating
f. Vowelizing

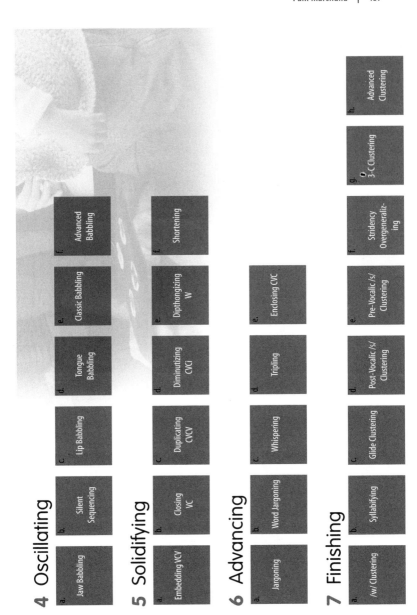

4 Oscillating

a. Jaw Babbling
b. Silent Sequencing
c. Lip Babbling
d. Tongue Babbling
e. Classic Babbling
f. Advanced Babbling

5 Solidifying

a. Embedding VCV
b. Closing VC
c. Duplicating CVCV
d. Diminutizing CVCi
e. Dipthongizing W
f. Shortening

6 Advancing

a. Jargoning
b. Word Jargoning
c. Whispering
d. Tripling
e. Enclosing CVC

7 Finishing

a. /w/ Clustering
b. Syllabifying
c. Glide Clustering
d. Post-Vocalic /s/ Clustering
e. Pre-Vocalic /s/ Clustering
f. Stridency Overgeneralizing
g. 3-C Clustering
h. Advanced Clustering

REFERENCES

Apraxia
Penelope Hall, Linda Jordan, Donald Robin; *Developmental Apraxia of Speech* (Austin, TX: Pro-Ed., 1993).

Pam Marshalla, *Becoming Verbal with Childhood Apraxia* (Kirkland, WA: Marshalla Speech and Language, 2000).

Feeding
Suzanne Evans Morris and Marsha Dunn Klein, *Pre-Feeding Skills* (Tuscon, AZ: Communication Skill Builders, 1988).

Infant Vocalizations
D. Kimbrough Oller, "Infant Vocalizations and the Development of Speech", *Allied Health and Behavioral Sciences Journal*, Volume 1, Number 14; p. 523-549.

Oral-Motor

Pam Marshalla, *Oral-Motor Techniques in Articulation and Phonological Therapy* (Kirkland, WA: Marshalla Speech and Language, 2000).

Phonetics

James Carrell and William R. Tiffany, *Phonetics: Theory and Application to Speech Improvement* (New York: McGraw-Hill Book Company, 1960).

Phonology

Barbara W. Hodson and Elaine Pagel Paden, *Targeting Intelligible Speech* (San Diego, CA: College-Hill Press, 1983).

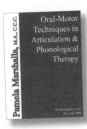